If a man's home is his castle, then how do you cook a moat?

by Peter Seymour

The C. R. Gibson Company • Norwalk, Connecticut

Copyright ©MCMLXXX by
The C. R. Gibson Company, Norwalk, Connecticut
All rights reserved
Printed in the United States of America
ISBN: 0-8378-3103-2

INTRODUCTION

If you're a man who has ever yelled **"HELP!"** when confronted with the new-found responsibilities of "keeping house"...this book is for you! It's chock full of dazzling ideas, basic information, hints, time savers, suggestions and, in general, a little inspiration (and just plain fun!) for *any* man who's on his own in a house, condo, apartment ...or even a tent! Make it an experience, be imaginative, have no fear! Remember, it's your very own place, enjoy it!

"He wore a pea-green coat, white vest, nankeen small clothes (breeches), white silk stockings, and pumps fastened with silver buckles which covered at least half the foot from instep to toe. His small clothes were tied at the knees with ribbon in double bows, the ends reaching to the ankle."

Description of a bachelor dandy,
Boston, ca. 1795

ODE TO A CHEF
"Amidst the din of party strife
Illustrious chef! you bare the knife
To save — not extinguish — life...
For place or pension many fight,
You only war with appetite!"

COOKING &

"A bachelor is a man who prefers to cook his own goose."

Or maybe his own chicken!

When you buy a fresh, ready to cook chicken or chicken parts, remove from package, wrap loosely in wax paper or foil, and keep in coldest part of your refrigerator.

Organizing the Kitchen

"Give me the provisions and whole apparatus of a kitchen, and I would still starve!"
                                    Montaigne

Many a bachelor has echoed that remark. The solution seems to be in the phrase KNOW THY KITCHEN! It is, after all, a place you can't avoid. So think of it as a place over which you have *total control*.

The kitchen takes a little more planning than any other part of your home. Once you've used it for a while, you'll begin to feel comfortable . . . and discover that you can't stand to have anyone else come in and try to tell you how to operate in it!

BASIC FOODS to have on hand....
This will, of course, vary with the kind of cooking and amount of eating you do at home. The following items I think you'll be glad to have on the premises:

All-purpose flour mix
  (for pancakes, biscuits)
Salt (and probably pepper)
Sugar
Noodles
Rice
Macaroni
Spaghetti
Potatoes
(and onions if you like them)
Butter (or margarine)
Cooking oil
Salad dressing
Mayonnaise
Catsup
Mustard
Cereal (hot and/or cold)
Canned soup
Tomato sauce
A few fruits and vegetables
Bread (perhaps crackers)
Favorite few spices
Coffee or Tea
  (if you drink 'em)
Syrup (or honey)
Frozen or canned juice
Pet food

OTHER KITCHEN ITEMS:
filters for coffee-maker
paper towels
napkins
aluminum foil
wax paper
soap
dish rag
scrub pads
dish washing liquid

Put together your own "Basic Shelf" of utensils based on your lifestyle, what you like to eat and how much cooking and entertaining you intend to do.

Here are what I would call just about the bare necessities:
Frying pan
   10-inch with a cover
One large pot
   (five quart or more)
Several smaller pots
   (also called saucepans)
A casserole or loaf pan
   (2 quart size)
Set of mixing bowls
A couple of cookie sheets
Measuring cup
   (2 cup size)
And measuring spoons

A colander or large strainer
Several good cutting knives
Electric mixer or egg beater
Spatulas — metal and plastic
   (for non-stick surfaces)
Can opener
Coffee pot

To this list add for more convenience:
Double boiler
Roasting pan
Tea kettle
Cheese/vegetable grater
Blender
Canister set
   (to store flour, sugar, etc.)
Chopping block or
   cutting board
Wooden spoons
Pancake griddle
Vegetable peeler

The oldest known can of food was found in a sunken British ship off the east coast of Canada; it was traced to the year 1823. What was in the can? Roast Beef!

A SHREWD SHOPPER

"It is probably common household knowledge by this time that I am one of the shrewdest shoppers of our time. The word gets around. When I enter a supermarket or a hardware store, there is a sudden hush every time, and then the customers fight to get as close to my little cart as they can. The effect is comparable to that which would be achieved if Nijinsky suddenly stepped out on the ballroom floor for a quick whirl."

George E. Condon

CAVEAT EMPTOR

CAVEAT EMPTOR!
That's Latin and it means "Let the Buyer Beware."
The Buyer — that's You!
With some practice, by observing and asking questions, you can become a smart shopper. TALK to the Produce Man, the Butcher, the Baker.
Look around. Compare.
Avoid getting stuck with a lemon... unless you're thirsty for lemonade.

Remember...

"Installment buying was invented to make the months seem shorter!"

"A budget is an orderly system for living beyond your means."

And "When your outgo exceeds your income, your upkeep is your downfall."

BASIC HINTS FOR FOOD SHOPPING:

Buy perishable foods in small amounts.
Write out a shopping list ... don't get home and find out you forgot that one "must" ingredient!
Check "sell by" or "use by" dates on cartons/containers, especially for dairy products.

"Buy not what you want but what you need."

Cato

In other words, don't go shopping when you're HUNGRY! Statistics show that your impulse buying will double or triple.

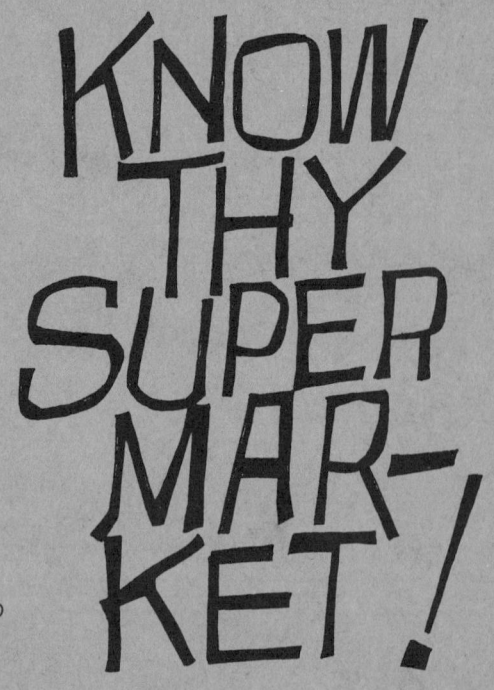

In the 1850's a typical country store had about 900 food items in stock. Today, a supermarket offers up to 10,000 items!

KNOW THY SUPERMARKET!

Get acquainted with the place or places you shop. Learn where things are... and you'll speed up the trip. Make friends with a produce person and a particular checker for more personal service. Establish check-cashing privilege.

Watch out for Shopping Basket Road Hogs!

Supermarket "house brands" are usually less money than "name" brands and are generally just as good.

Don't forget the "Quick Checkout" lane — 10 items or less. Be prepared for it to be full of cheaters — including yourself at times. I mean, eleven or twelve items is *almost* ten, right?

Need to save money? Let yourself *run out* of things. You'll be surprised how you can get along without 'em for a while!

When you buy a small bottle of flavoring — vanilla, orange, almond, etc. — the label should say "pure." Such flavor extracts taste better than those marked "artificial," which are created from chemicals.

Closets were unknown before 1800. People hung clothing on pegs in the open, or kept their clothes in trunks.

"This is the way we
    wash our clothes,
      wash our clothes,
        wash our clothes,
This is the way we
    wash our clothes
      on a Monday morning."
            Old Nursery Rhyme

Well...
it's more
like on a
Saturday for
the modern
bachelor!

DOING THE LAUNDRY

In the good old days most single guys had to lug their dirty duds and sheets, towels and what-have-you to the laundromat... where many a romance was born! Alas, nowadays a washer and dryer are right on the premises where you live, where you're less likely to run into the motherly type who will tell you far more than you ever wanted to know about doing the laundry. Still, there are a few hints to consider:

Test colored clothing to see if it *runs* before mixing it in with other wash.

Generally wash white stuff by itself.

Never add bleach when washing colored things . . . unless you're purposely going for the faded look.

Don't overload the washing machine. It won't work as it should, may tangle your stuff up and even tear it, and possibly not get rid of the ring-around-the-collar either.

Measure the amount of soap or detergent, as instructed. Too many suds can keep your clothes from agitating properly and thus mean they won't get as clean as they should.

Be sure the detergent is *dissolved* in the water *before* you cram your clothes into the washer! Undissolved detergent might eat at and fade your clothes if, like almost all the men I know, you sprinkle it on top of your clothes, after they're in the machine!

Editorial reprinted from the Nurnville *Daily Bugle:*
"Should single men work? Should working men keep house?" These, and similar questions — for example, "Should married women work outside the home?" and "Should working women cook?" — have about as much relevance today as engine cranks for Model T's.
The answer to such questions is obviously "Yes!" In terms of *single* men who decide to keep house for themselves, socio-psychologists would doubtless say that it will help develop their personalities to the fullest and give them an added sense of self-worth!

HOW TO PUT MORE TIME IN YOUR LIFE:

sleep less than you do
read less of the morning (or evening) paper
leave for work later (or earlier) to miss the worst traffic (same goes for coming home)
make fewer (and shorter) phone calls
cut down on visits to the barber shop, the grocery store, the gas station, the post office — and the local bar! Seriously, a little planning *can* cut down on the number of time-wasting trips you make. Of course, some guys are into making lots of little trips — because they can't think of how else to spend their time.

Remember the words of Omar Khayyam: "The Bird of Time has but a little way to flutter — and the Bird is on the Wing!"

THE "WAKE-UP" BED...
is a combination of hard wood, hinges, springs, and clock-work. If, for instance, you set the hand **A** for six, in the morning at six o'clock at the bed's head solemnly strikes a demi-twelve on its sonorous bell **B**. If you pay no attention to the monitor ... the invention within two minutes drops its tail-board **C** and lets down your feet upon the floor. (Then) the virtuous head-board and the rest of the bed suddenly rise up in protest; and the next moment **D** if you do not instantly abdicate, you are launched upon the floor by a blind elbow that connects to a crank **E** that is turned by a cord **F** that is wound around a drum ...

Concocted by
Fred S. Cozzens, ca. 1850

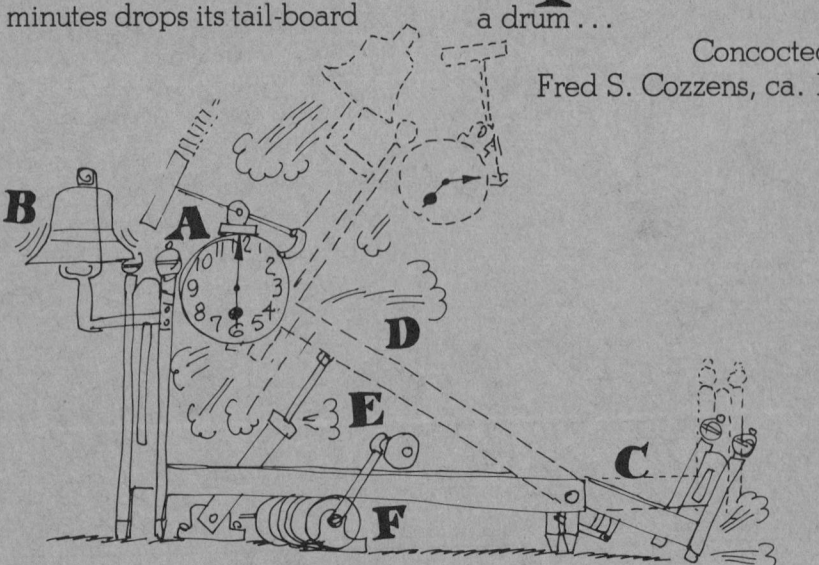

RISE AND SHINE

sluggard

"*Sluggard*—why, it is a calling and vocation, it is a career!"

Dostoevsky

TRY THIS: Plug your electric coffee pot (filled with water and coffee) into a timer device set so that the coffee will be perked whenever you wish—in concert with your alarm clock, after your shower, when you're all dressed. The coffee aroma may also help you wake up!

Bleary-eyed thought: Superstition has it that if you accidentally put a piece of clothing on inside out, it's an omen of good luck!

However: if you button a button in the wrong buttonhole, look out!

Most men I know have worked out their own little techniques for getting from bed to job as efficiently as possible.
The methods vary, from having clothes all laid out the night before, to skipping breakfast!
A friend of mine always took his shower the night before. Another guy liked soft-boiled eggs: he discovered they cooked in exactly the time it took him to shave.
Another fellow I call "Cautious Charlie" kept extra belts, ties, handkerchiefs in his car.
Everyone can use a few extra winks... so think of ways *you* can streamline your morning get-away activities.

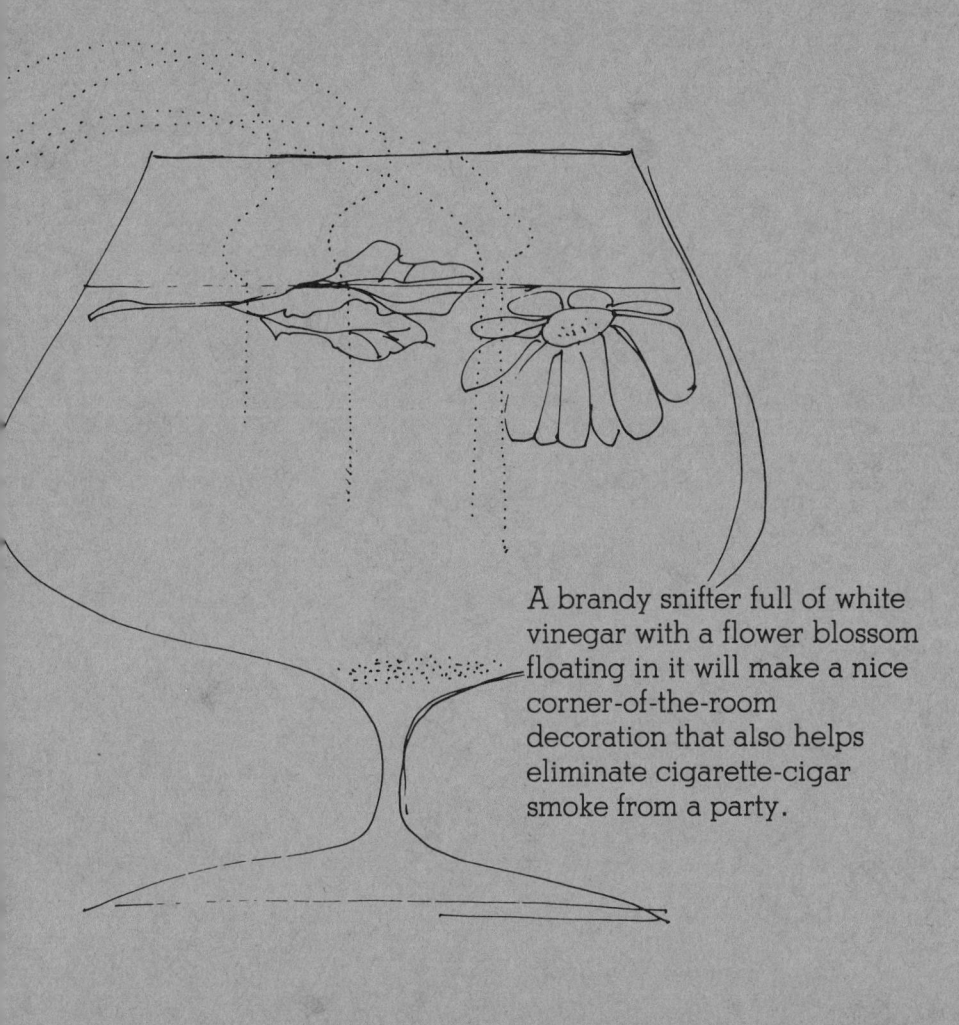

A brandy snifter full of white vinegar with a flower blossom floating in it will make a nice corner-of-the-room decoration that also helps eliminate cigarette-cigar smoke from a party.

Cover an old telephone book with foil and it becomes a hot-pot stand ... and may save your kitchen counter top from a few scorches and burns.

A woven plastic berry basket can substitute for a small collander.

Warning!
Don't try to unclog a sink drain with a wire coat hanger! I tried it once and the wire went right through the pipe.

Wear gloves to unscrew a broken light bulb ... and to pick up broken glass.

Glass window panes appeared in Venice and Genoa around the 13th century... but they were so rare that people took them with them when they moved!

Line the bottom of your garbage sack with aluminum foil to keep the sack from bursting if the garbage is wet.

A plastic coffee can lid can substitute for a sink stopper.

In the 18th century, bayberry-scented candles were so popular that laws were enacted limiting the "season" when the berries and leaves could be picked.

The first practical friction matches were made in England in 1827. Eighty-four came in a box and cost 25¢.

The rocking chair was invented in America ca. 1775.

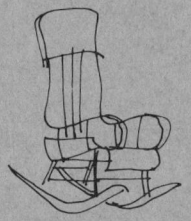

To hammer in a nail without hammering your thumb and fingers: first stick nail through a strip of cardboard... and hold onto the cardboard rather than the nail.

When you have a "sticky" door, try tacking a piece of sandpaper between it and the floor or door jamb. Open and close the door for self-sanding... and avoid removing the door!

Good stuff to have around

Along with the usual hammer,
wrench, screwdriver and
flashlight, it's wise and often
wonderful to have on hand
several kinds of tape
(masking,
cellophane,
electrician's)
string
rope
a yardstick
tape measure
faucet washers
a funnel
work gloves
assorted nails
and screws
picture wire
and metal hangers
tacks
a little can of lubricating oil
putty knife or scraper
sandpaper
several good scissors
stapler (and staples)
fuses

Among the items you hate to
be out of when you really
need them:
light bulbs and batteries
   (for flashlight
   transistor
   calculator
   electronic game).
Also, paper clips
rubber bands
writing paper and
envelopes
stamps
matches
your favorite beverage
toilet paper
clean socks....

Don't forget 3-way bulbs
... they can give light when
you need it ... and
atmosphere when you want it!

"All things have their place, knew we how to place them."

George Herbert

VALUABLE PAPERS

I suggest you use a safety deposit box. However, few people do, and even *if* you do, there are all kinds of important papers (or semi-important) to deal with where you aren't going to run to the bank every day. Select *one single place* — a drawer, a shoe box under the bed, a briefcase — where you always put any and every single bit and piece of paper you think may be important to your life whenever one surfaces. Now and then sort out what you've accumulated and *get rid* of what's no longer important.

STORAGE SPACE?

Who isn't!

Add shelves to a closet that has none (or can take more).

Hang a shoe bag on the back of a closet door — for shoes as well as to hold all sorts of other things (light bulbs, string, extension cords, film, tools, etc.)

Use an old trunk for a coffee table (and as storage space for sheets and blankets). You can refinish the trunk or paint it to match your decor.

Baskets to hold things can be hung on closet walls or doors.

Small (or sometimes large) hooks on the backs of doors will hold belts, a bathrobe, a coat, vacuum cleaner attachments.

When storage becomes an impossible problem, give away everything you don't absolutely need to charity and get a nice tax deduction!

Know where **UTILITIES TURN OFF** (and on) — the Water . . . Gas . . . Electricity.

Locate circuit breakers or fuse box (and have extra fuses on hand). Don't ever use a penny.

Have emergency utility company numbers by the telephone.

In olden days in New England, the annual housecleaning often became a "Whang!" — a gathering of a few neighbors to help one another with that terrible chore.

The word "broom" is the name of a shrub which people used to tie together, making a thing to sweep with. Turkey wings were also used as sweepers in the good old days!

Boxes Are Best

For me,  are terrific for organizing storage space.
Boxes go under the bed, in closets and drawers, and on shelves — out of sight, but easy to get to.
And **BOXES** come in all sizes to fit various needs.
My jogging gear is in a medium-sized **BOX** shoe shine items in a shoe box; basketball, frizbee and other sports equipment in a

With your things organized by **BOX** you know where to put them . . . and more important, where to *find* 'em!

Remember — don't just put it down . . . put it *away!*

"I am inclined to think bathing almost one of the necessaries of life, but it is surprising how indifferent some are to it."

Thoreau

THE BATHROOM

Well, in those days a shower meant it was raining, and the soap you used was liable to take off not only the dirt but seven layers of skin, too!

But times change. Bathrooms are better than ever. The fact is, you spend more time in there than you think — so why not make it as inviting as possible.

And keep it clean!

Stick up a paper cup dispenser by the sink. It's more sanitary than using a glass ... and doesn't a glass always eventually get broken?

If you use a shower curtain ... use two of them. You'll keep more water out of the bathroom and more steam inside the shower. The outside curtain can be decorative or colorful, the inside one plain and practical.

Mildew: You can't stop it ... but you can slow it down by washing the inside shower curtain occasionally and wiping it with chlorine bleach.

A friend of mine has an item purchased at a department store that is terrific for saving soap in the shower: It is slightly larger than a bar of soap and has little suction cups on *both* sides. Stick it on the wall at the opposite end from the shower head; stick soap onto it to keep soap dry when you're not using it.

Shower doors need to be washed too ... and the sliding tracks cleaned out on sliding doors.

Put up a small hook on your bathroom door to hang your watch, ring, bracelet, etc. on if you don't want 'em to get wet or soapy.

The most useful item I've found for bathroom clean-up is a nice big sponge.

Occasionally check the timing gear on your mouse traps.

Don't leave old batteries in flashlight, calculator, camera, TV game, etc. They will leak, make a mess and sometimes even ruin the works.

SMALL
may be Just What You Need: remember that many appliances — washers, dryers, dishwashers, refrigerators, ranges — come in compact sizes to fit campers and boats . . . and small apartments, to give you more room!

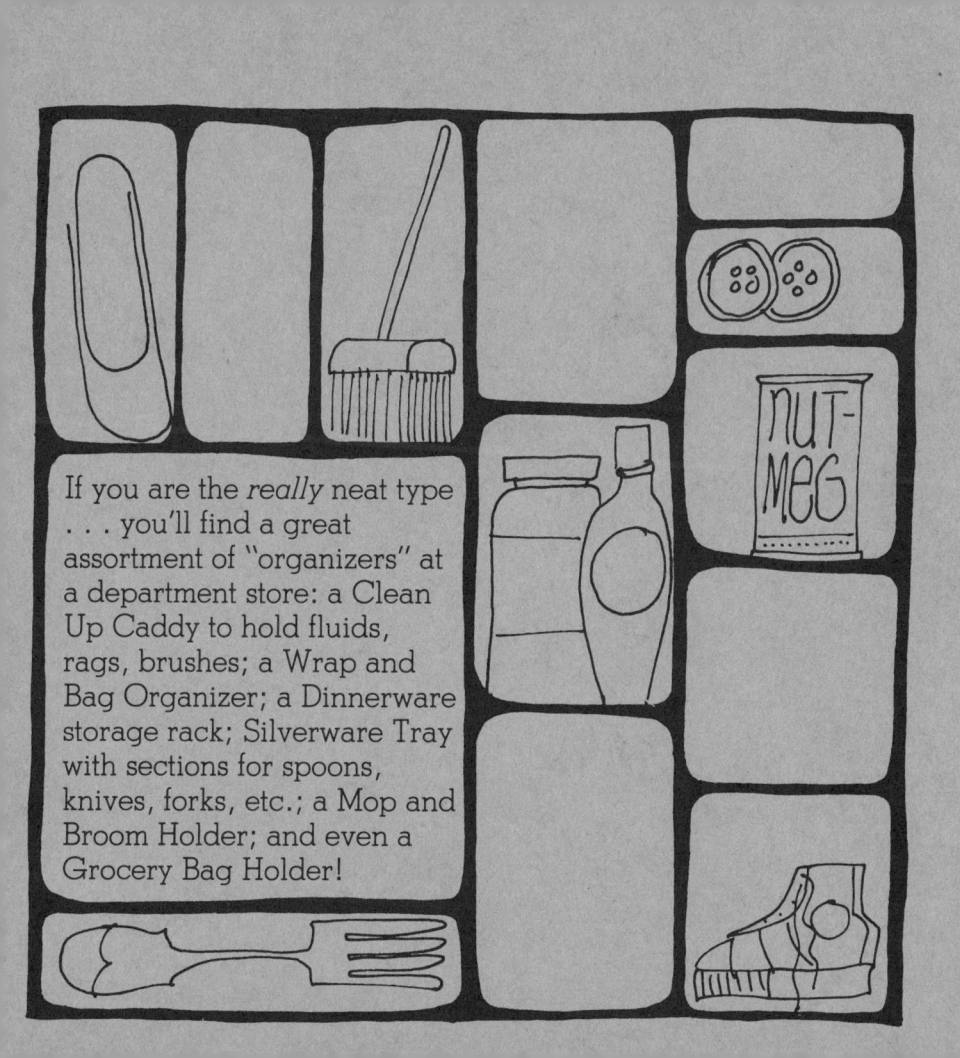

If you are the *really* neat type . . . you'll find a great assortment of "organizers" at a department store: a Clean Up Caddy to hold fluids, rags, brushes; a Wrap and Bag Organizer; a Dinnerware storage rack; Silverware Tray with sections for spoons, knives, forks, etc.; a Mop and Broom Holder; and even a Grocery Bag Holder!

In Georgia, in 1735, you could buy a whole deer from the Indians for sixpence.

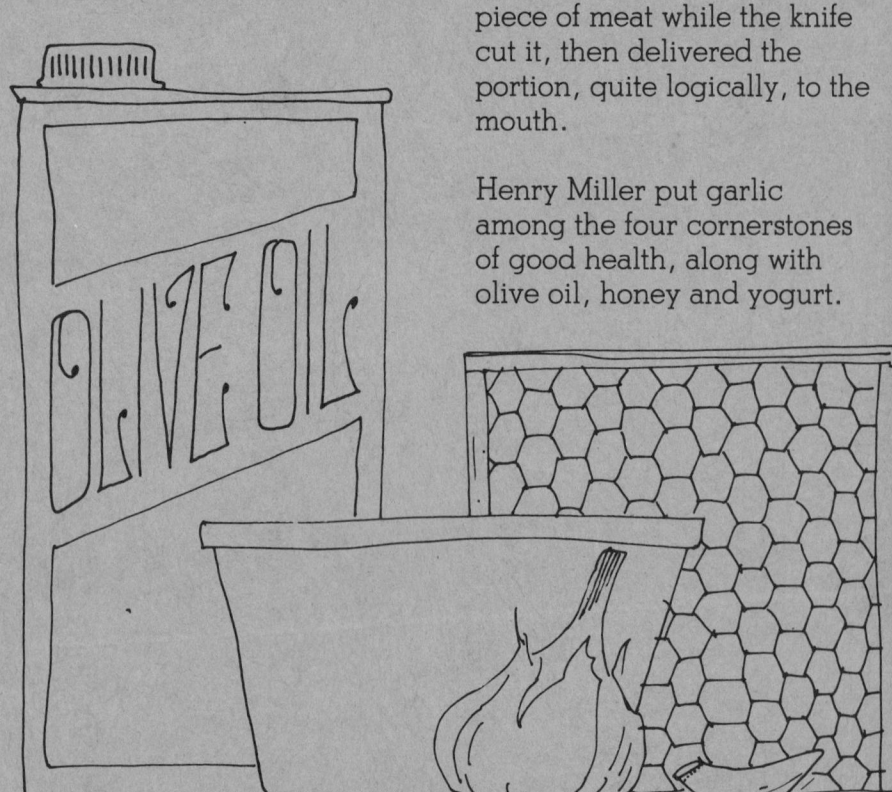

People used to eat with *knives* — and it was perfectly proper! The fork held down a piece of meat while the knife cut it, then delivered the portion, quite logically, to the mouth.

Henry Miller put garlic among the four cornerstones of good health, along with olive oil, honey and yogurt.

"Bachelor's fare: bread, cheese and kisses!"

Jonathan Swift

What is there to tell you about bread? If you care to be thrifty, buy a bunch of loaves at a "day-old" bakery outlet and freeze 'em. They thaw out fresh as new.

A piece of bread put on top of your rice after it's cooked (and still in the pot) will make it extra dry and fluffy.

As for kisses, bet you're already an expert.

. . . a few bits of information for the would-be gourmet . . . or if you just want a few trivia facts for the next quiz.

cheese

Camembert:
a soft cheese which should be softened further at room temp before serving. You can eat the thin, whitish crust. Serve for dessert, with salads, as all-purpose with fruits and crackers.

Edam:
comes usually in a red coating. It's mild, slightly salty, great as an appetizer or for dessert; serve in wedges. *Gouda,* also in red cover, is similar but stronger in taste, sometimes softer.

Roquefort:
comes with yellowish-brown rind. Inside it's white with blue-green mold, spicy flavor. It's great with fruit, crackers, in salads, crumbled with sour cream to make a dip or spread.

One of the wedding presents for Queen Victoria of England was an eleven-hundred pound cheese!

The holes in Swiss cheese are called "eyes." The eyes are formed by natural gases bubbling inside the cheese during its aging period of several months in a warm cellar.

eggs

When you buy a carton of eggs, always open it first and check to see that none of the eggs are broken or cracked.

nuts

Store unopened bags or cans of nuts in the refrigerator.

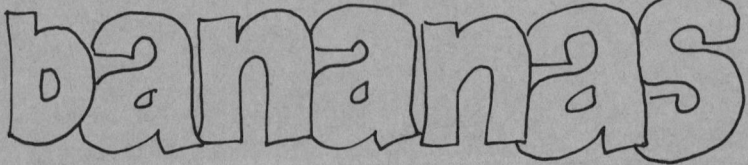

bananas

Buy bananas that are more green than yellow. They will ripen at room temp, and you'll be more likely to get them eaten before one or two spoil, or get so mushy you can't stand them.

coffee

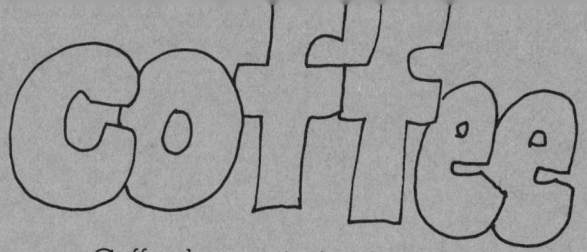

Coffee beans start out green. They are heated at very high temperatures and turn various shades of brown, to almost black.

A "Demitasse" is a tiny cup of coffee that you hold with your little finger pointing out.

Keep opened coffee can *tightly* sealed. Air quickly destroys flavor. Try to use up an opened can within a week.

Keep opened coffee can in the refrigerator.

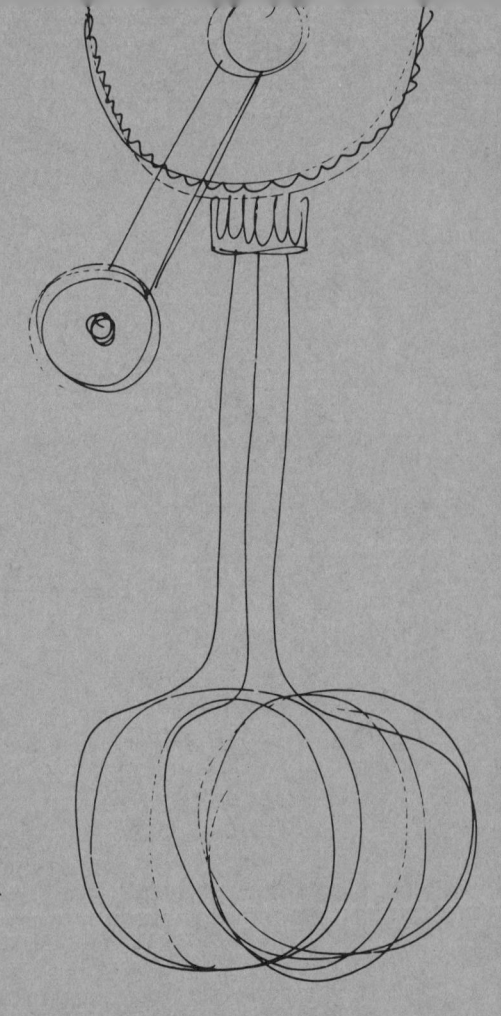

If you're having trouble getting cream to whip, add a few drops of lemon juice or a pinch of plain gelatin powder.

For smoother spaghetti sauce, throw all the ingredients into a blender before cooking or heating the sauce.

If you have an electric frying pan, you can pop corn in it!

Try making French toast in your waffle iron. Do not make pancakes in your waffle iron, however.

Like broccoli . . . but the stems are always tough? Slice the stems a couple of times all the way up into the flower portion before cooking.

brown meat

Brown meat quicker and better: first pat meat *dry* with paper towel and then be sure fat or oil is *very hot*.

butter toast

Butter toast or rolls on a piece of paper towel; discard towel, leaving no mess on counter and no plate to wash.

When you cook, act like a fool: wear an apron! Things do spill, grease does splatter.

bacon

Try frying bacon criss-crossed in pan next time you need to fry a lot at once; turn the whole thing at once with a large spatula.

S&P

How to fill salt and pepper shakers that fill from the *bottom:* Put cellophane tape over the holes before you turn the shaker over.

FAT ON FIRE

Never put a loaf of bread on the table upside down: the Devil will fly over your house!

The FAT caught on FIRE! Quick — turn off the burner. Use fire extinguisher if you have one.
OR pour on baking soda or salt or smother fire with pot lid.
Do NOT throw on flour; it might explode.

YOU MIGHT AS WELL LEARN A LITTLE OF THE LANGUAGE!

cooking terms

Baste:
to put liquid over food while it's cooking, usually refers to roast or turkey, using its own juices.

Blanche:
to pour very hot (usually boiling) water over food to loosen skin, such as almonds or tomatoes.

Braise:
to brown food, usually meat, in a little fat or oil, then add liquid and cook in covered pan.

Coddle:
to cook slowly and just below the boiling point.

Cream:
nothing to do with your coffee — to mix butter or shortening with a spoon, usually, against sides of a bowl, until it's really smooth, that is "creamy!"

Dredge:
to coat with flour, or sometimes sugar or cheese or ground-up topping like bread crumbs.

Glacé:
to coat with sugar syrup — rather elegant!

Grease:
to rub a pan or dish, or a potato, with shortening.

Julienne:
to cut in long, thin strips, as with potatoes or meat.

Knead:
what you used to do as a kid with clay — only now you do it with dough if you're interested in baking.

Marinate:
(sometimes Marinade): to soak food for a while in some sort of flavorful liquid, which is, correctly speaking, the Marinade.

Sauté:
to fry in a pan in a small amount of fat.

Score:
we all know what that means! Oh — in cooking, it means to cut little grooves in the surface of food.

by Arnold J. Nurnbolt
Socio-psychologist

WHY DO *MEN* KEEP HOUSE?

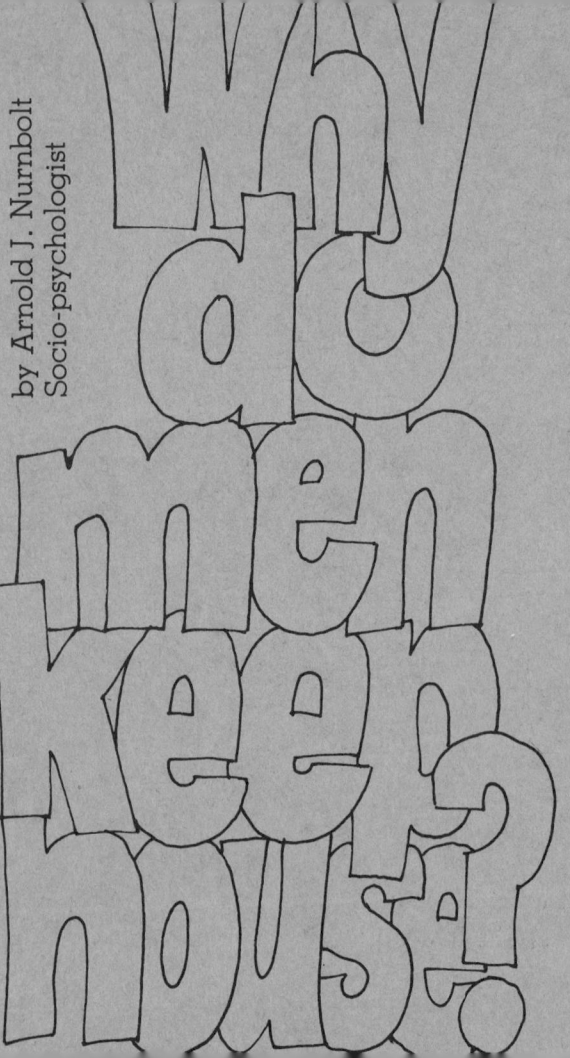

Why do men keep house? For many reasons, I think. Some men have no choice. They have a "clean it" fixation. They badly need to remove garbage, wash socks, change a sheet. Others simply want raise their standard of living Others like to be alone: their jobs are too full of noise and people-chatter; doing housework provides those quiet, reflective times. A few men find the repetitious, routine nature of housework is good therapy. They are n prepared for a life of freedo and no discipline. Housewo offers security, in other words. And then there are men who are fed up with the glamour of the outside world They are into drudgery in a big way and love the tediou chores of sweeping floors ar washing windows. Finally, some men are burdened with the ethical and moral implications of housework and must keep house in order to avoid guilt.

house cleaning

Look in the Yellow Pages under "House Cleaning!" You can get set up for once-a-week (if you're moneybags). Or once every two weeks or once a month . . . even once a year.

Most men do-it-themselves, of course — with an occasional "Big Sweep" from friends, relatives or a professional cleaning company.

Whatever you do, don't try to clean draperies or furniture. You can get pros to do it right in your house or apartment.

When dusting, use both hands — a dust cloth in each — to save time (and give your arms an equal work-out). If you're really ambitious, strap mops to both feet!

DETAILS ON DUST

Men new to the housecleaning game are often surprised to learn about DUST.

Oh, they knew dust was on the floor and under the bed. But they seldom thought to look elsewhere.
For example:
- on light bulbs
- the TV screen
- lamp shades
- the leaves of indoor plants
- the telephone
- chair and table legs
- books
- the record player
- decorative candles
- picture frames
- seldom-used dishes and glasses
- behind range and refrigerator
- along tops of doors and window sills
- in the ice bucket

"Above all things, keep clean. It is not necessary to be a pig to raise one."

Robert Ingersoll

But don't get paranoid about it! You'll have to decide what's clean enough . . . at any given time or for any particular occasion.

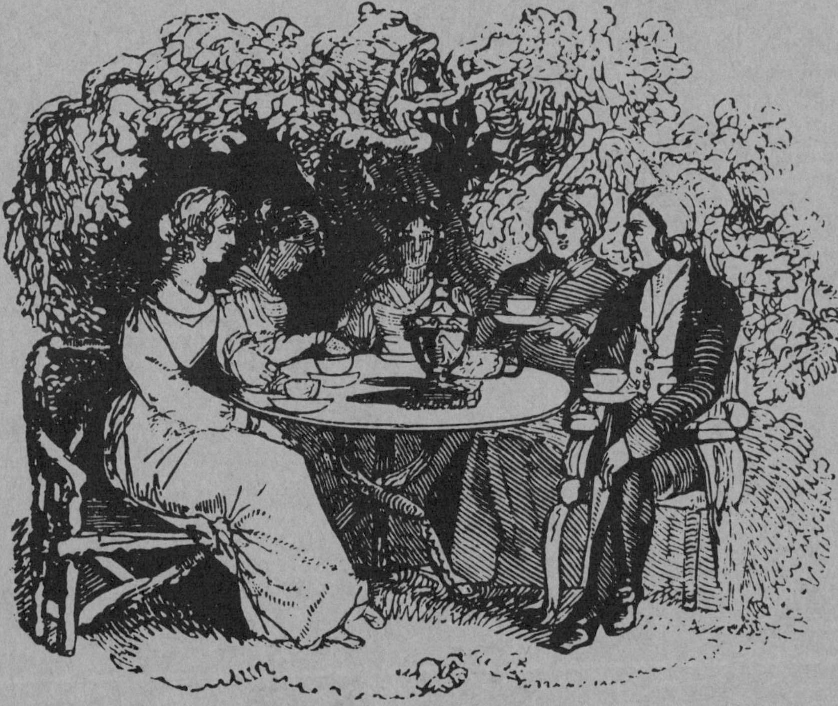

"The trouble in civilized life of entertaining *company,* as it is called too generally without much regard to strict veracity, is so great that it cannot but be a matter of wonder that people are so fond of attempting it!"

Trollope

"A cocktail party is a gathering where olives are speared and friends stabbed."

The best advice to anyone who is going to have one person or three dozen people over is to *be prepared!*

be prepared

Set the table ahead of time.
Decide on seating.
Arrange chairs.
Have ice, glasses, liquor, mixers, olives, lemon, a knife, spoon, etc. all out in one place (wherever you make your bar) ready to go.
Have napkins and coasters available.
If it's cold weather (or any weather where guests will have coats), the bedroom is

the usual place to stash them — so don't forget to clean up your bedroom!
If you plan music in the background, get your tapes and/or records organized.

Two nights leftovers plan it right

Consider entertaining a different friend, or group of friends, two nights in a row — or maybe with one night off in between. I know a fellow who has done this and come out ahead in terms of time, effort and cost. You'll have a lot of leftovers from the first affair — not only booze, crackers, cheese and other food that's still useable, but candles, perhaps fresh flowers or other decorations. If you plan it right, you can get by with only one big shopping trip, too.

hors d'oeuvres

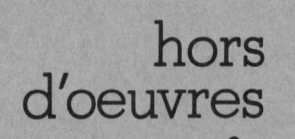

Bacon Snacks
Cut bacon slices in half, fry for about 5 minutes (but don't let 'em get crisp). Then wrap them around any of a variety of items and hold with toothpicks: dates, olives, cocktail franks, sautéed chicken livers, etc.
Bake on a cookie sheet at 400° for ten minutes.

Avocado Dip

Into a blender put: 2 cut-up avocados, the juice of one lemon, an 8 oz. pack of softened cream cheese, a dash of tabasco sauce. After blending, if it seems too "stiff" add a bit of milk and blend some more.

Seafood Dip

Begin with 4 oz. softened cream cheese, 4 oz. sour cream, juice of one lemon, 1½ teaspoons worcestershire sauce, a tablespoon of mayonnaise, a hint of garlic salt . . . mix into smoothness in blender.

To this add whatever kind of seafood you want — cut into tiny pieces — minced clams, crab meat, shrimp, salmon, etc.

Punch and a Few Less Known Drink Recipes (the recipes, not the drinks!)

WINE COOLER

1 quart burgundy
1 cup sugar
4 oranges and 4 lemons (or 2 lemons, 2 limes) sliced up.

Heat the wine, but don't boil it.

Add the fruit and sugar. Stir over low heat to dissolve sugar. Let cool, then serve with ice. You might want to add some soda water. Also, add more wine to taste!
Above recipe makes about 6 five-ounce servings.

CHAMPAGNE-BRANDY PUNCH

Mix in a large bowl over ice: 4 oz. of lemon and 4 oz. of pineapple juice; 8 oz. of brandy and 3 oz. of grenadine; one bottle of white wine, chablis would be best. Just before you're ready to serve, pour in two cold bottles of champagne. Makes 32 servings.

Make ice cubes faster by leaving 2 or 3 cubes *in the tray* when you fill it with water.

For something different, try offering these drinks. In my experience women like them, but men don't usually know how to make them.

GRASSHOPPER
In a shaker put 1 part each creme de menthe, white creme de cacao and cream. Shake with cracked ice, serve.

FROZEN DAIQUIRI
Use whatever fruit you want — strawberries, peaches, sliced up apples. Mix in a blender 3 oz. white rum, juice of 1 lime, half a cup of fruit, 3 tablespoons of fruit syrup (if frozen fruit; if fresh, add a tablespoon of sugar) and some cracked ice. Blend for 10 seconds.

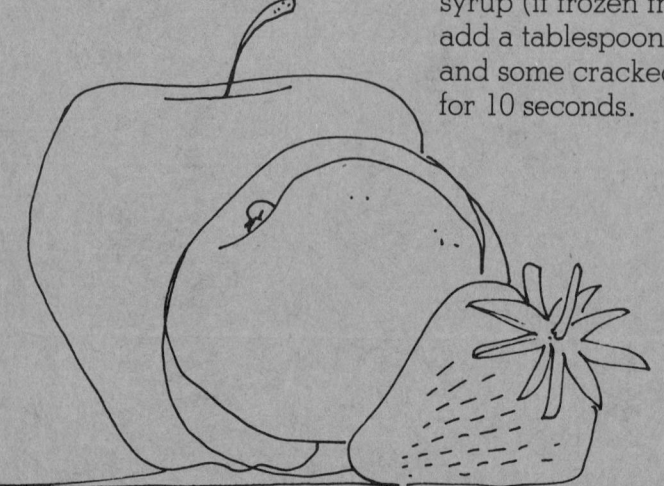

If you plan to serve punch, freeze some of it in ice trays (without the liquor in it, if you're having alcoholic punch). Add "punched up" ice cubes to keep punch cold without diluting flavor.

> "He bids the ruddy cup go round
> Till sense and sorrow both are drowned."
>
> Sir Walter Scott

Don't buy, serve or drink a cheap champagne!

Hardly anyone pays any attention anymore to whether you serve red or white wine with meat, fish or fowl. It's a matter of taste.

According to gourmets, having a cold drink before a good meal is ridiculous; the cold deadens the taste buds. One suggestion: serve a hot soup as the first course!

A gourmet would suggest that you drink (and serve) before dinner an aperitif wine such as a dry sherry or dry vermouth. Add a twist of lemon.

Cocktails: the smart fellows I know insist it is the *quality* of the *mixers* rather than the booze itself that makes the difference in creating an outstanding drink. So whether it's vermouth, tonic, soda, olives, fruit — whatever — get the very best you can.

What do you drink from? A good investment is

a selection

for various kinds of drinking. You don't have to go overboard with this... but why not go for

a basic cocktail glass   an old fashioned glass

# of glasses

plain highball

wine

brandy snifter

"Let us have wine and women, mirth and laughter!"

Lord Byron

The most popular German white wine in the U. S. is Liebfraumilch.

Don't serve champagne in colored glasses — it takes away from the color and quality of the champagne itself.

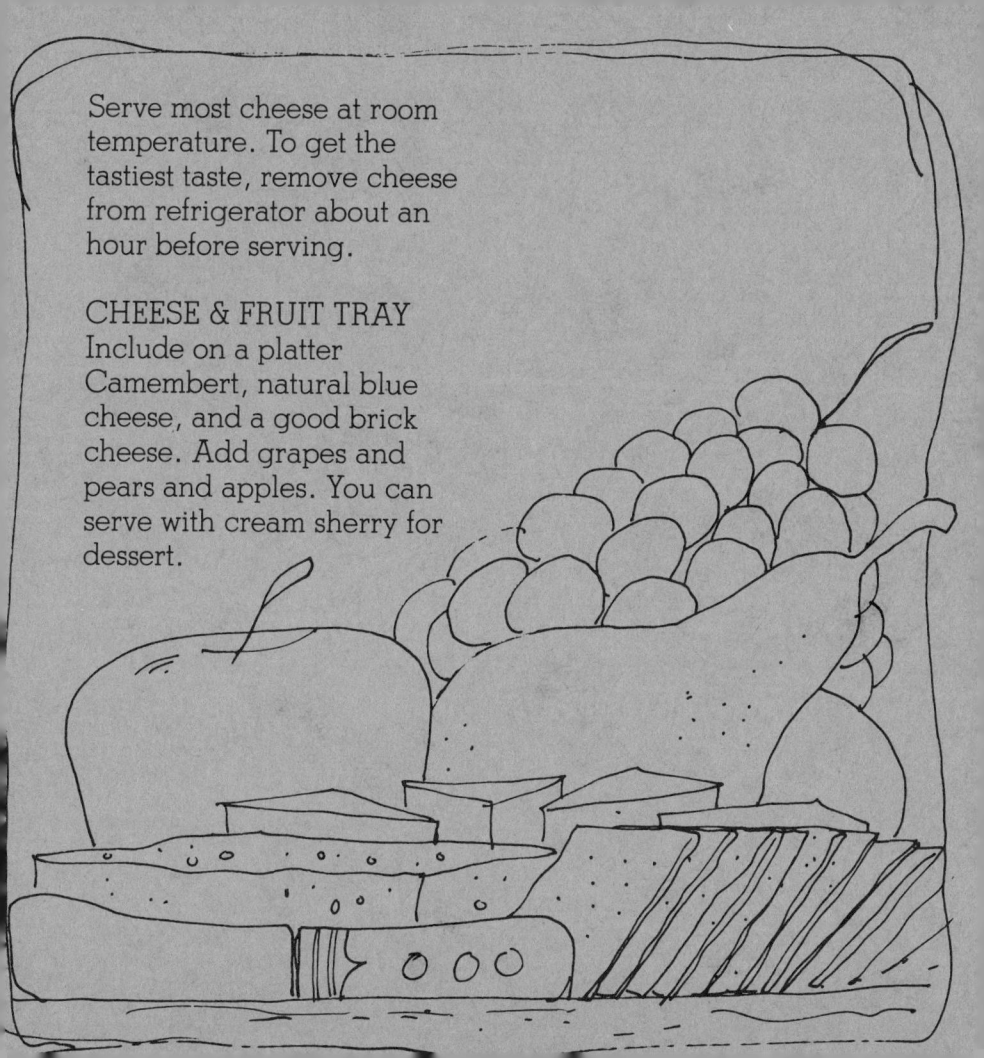

Serve most cheese at room temperature. To get the tastiest taste, remove cheese from refrigerator about an hour before serving.

CHEESE & FRUIT TRAY

Include on a platter Camembert, natural blue cheese, and a good brick cheese. Add grapes and pears and apples. You can serve with cream sherry for dessert.

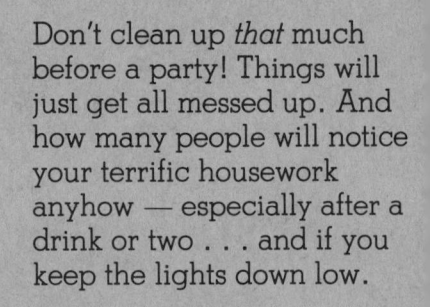

Don't clean up *that* much before a party! Things will just get all messed up. And how many people will notice your terrific housework anyhow — especially after a drink or two . . . and if you keep the lights down low.

If one of your candles sputters, says my superstitious pal, it means a stranger will arrive (probably a party crasher or your girl friend's ex-boyfriend).

AFTER THE PARTY

Scratches and blemishes on wood: rub in furniture wax with fine steel wool very gently, then polish. Try using magic-marker type pen in an appropriate color to cover scratch.

Candle wax: apply ice cube for a few seconds, wipe up melted water at once, carefully scratch off with fingernail or dull knife (repeat ice process as needed); polish with wax.

Water mark: place thick blotter over the mark and press with a warm iron.

Alcohol spots or white spots or rings: try rubbing the blemish with some cigarette ashes and a cloth dipped in salad oil (or cream wax, if you have it), or use a little salt instead of ashes. Always wipe thoroughly and polish.

"Home is home, be it never so homely."

Charles Dickens

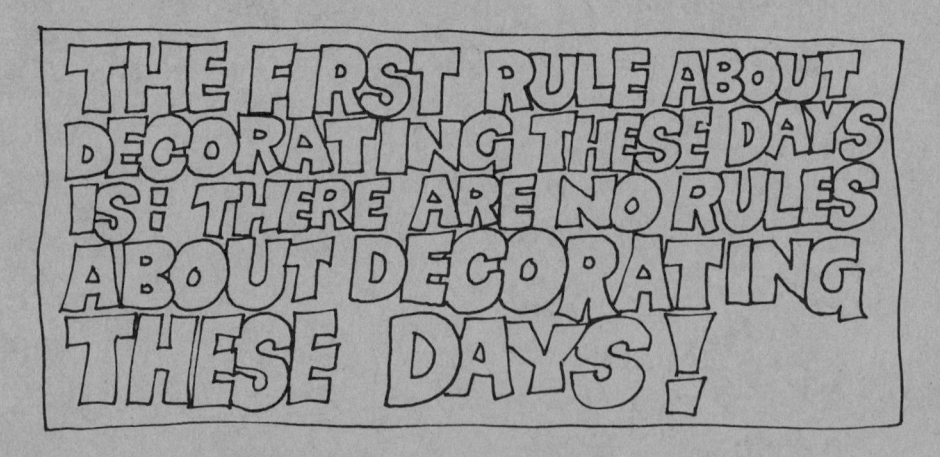

THE FIRST RULE ABOUT DECORATING THESE DAYS IS: THERE ARE NO RULES ABOUT DECORATING THESE DAYS!

You have a lot of freedom . . . which is liable to make you nervous!

If you're moving into a new place . . . or are tired with your present one and contemplate "redoing it" as they say — wait: don't rush into things. Take your time. Do it right. And for Heaven's sake, don't worry about having company over while you're still in the midst of decorating. They might have a good suggestion!
But . . . don't decorate to please someone else. Please yourself!

If your living room area is small, avoid large pieces of furniture and don't crowd too much into it.

For a change of pace, cover a couch or easy chair with a light-weight bedspread of an unusual print, fabric or color.

Use different sized and shaped pillows to accent your couch or seating arrangement.

Walls can be fun! Consider them big empty spaces to play with. Wallpaper one wall only of a room. Look for unusual frames for your favorite pictures. If you have a particular hobby that lends itself to framing (collecting stamps, a restaurant's unique menu, for example) use it as a decorative touch.

Repainting your walls isn't as big a deal as it may seem. The water-based, latex paints and rollers make the job go fast, and it isn't messy any more. Consider a flat white or light colored paint . . . which will give you an all-purpose background for whatever furniture, carpet or wall decor you have or will get. Consult a paint store salesperson for the best type of paint and equipment to use for your particular needs.

You can get rid of fresh paint odor in a room if you put an onion, cut in half, in a pan of water in the room.

"A man's bedroom should be masterful without looking aggressive — bold, if you will, and full of personality, but not noticeably fresh."

Will Cuppy

I would agree with that . . . and only add it should also be

DARK!

Invest in some good *blackout* shades for sleeping . . . but don't forget to raise them in the morning!

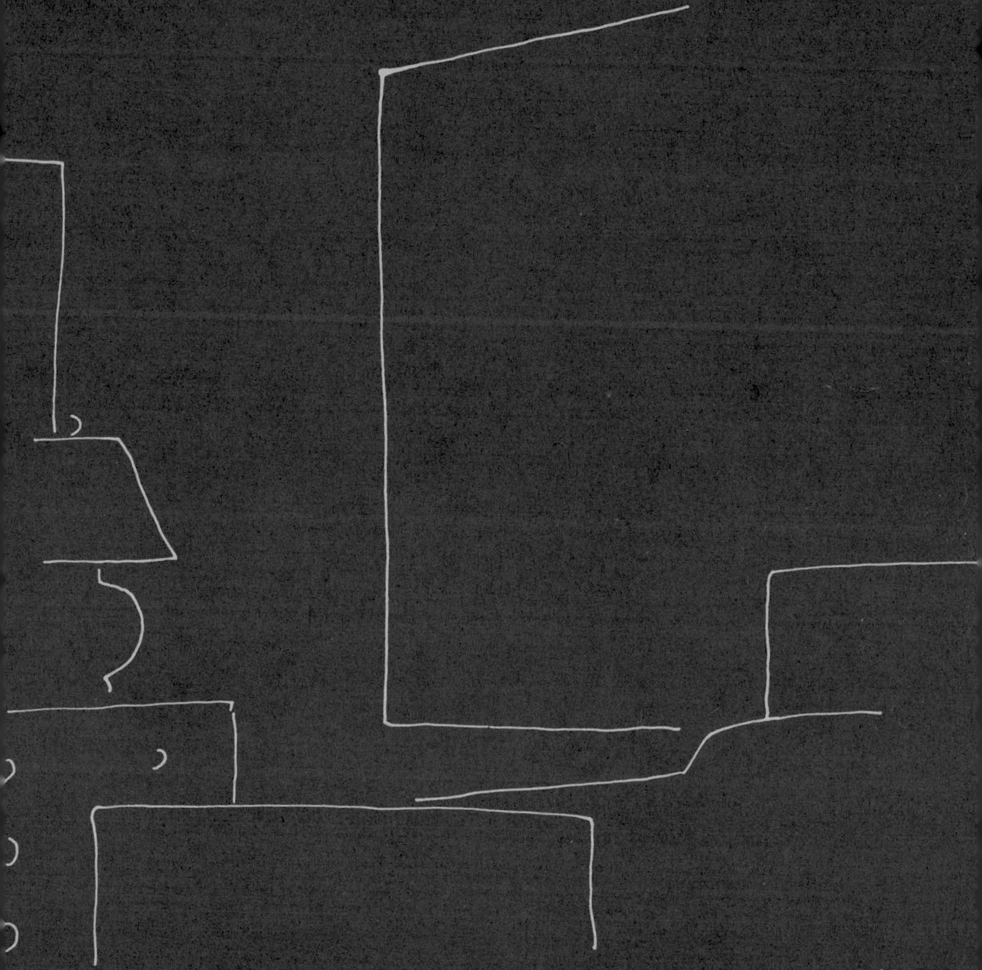

Did You Know . . .

Perhaps the most famous bed in the world is the "Great Bed of Ware," in Shakespeare's *Twelfth Night,* which is now in Hertfordshire, England. It is 12 feet square, with elaborate carvings in the headboard, the posts and the "roof" or canopy. It slept 12 people!

"Sanitary Engineering" appeared just before the turn of the century; at that time, pipes were made out of lead (wooden pipes were manufactured as late as 1875) and sinks and bathtubs were wooden boxes lined with lead sheets.

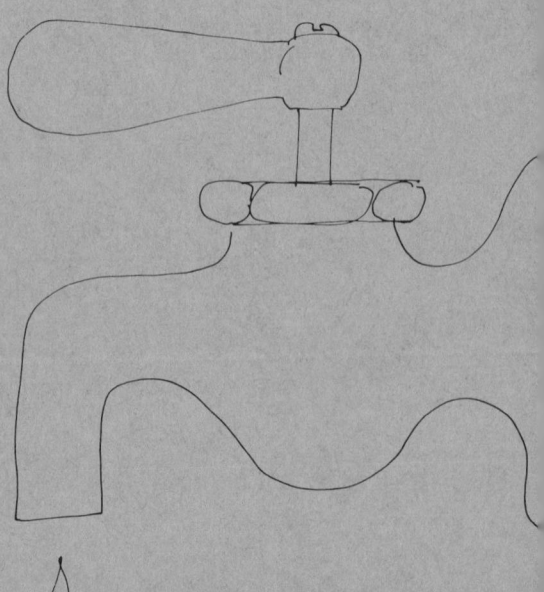

"The discovery of a new dish does more for the happiness of man than the discovery of a star."

Brillat-Savarin

Never heat an unopened can . . . it might **EXPLODE**

Don't buy (or use the contents of) a can that has swelled up. The food inside is probably spoiled . . . and could spoil you! Contrary to popular belief, a *dented* can is okay (and often on sale at a discount).

OPENING A CAN IS A CAN ... OR IS IT?

One secret to very simple but tasty cooking is to *add* ingredients to canned or frozen or already prepared foods. This method beats a steady diet of TV dinners, and is almost as quick.

To cans of cream-style soups (such as mushroom), instead of using all milk or water, substitute some dry white wine. Heat slowly on low flame, stirring occasionally; don't let it boil! And don't drink too much of the wine (at least while you're fixing the soup).

add

To canned spaghetti, ravioli, lasagne, etc., add grated cheese (whatever you like) and a small can of tomato paste; you can also add a few sliced mushrooms . . . or be otherwise creatively Italian! Oregano, garlic powder. . . .

Heat canned vegetables in butter and add spices.

mix

Mix canned fruits — say, peaches, apricots, cherries — and make a compote, either cold or heated.

Mix canned sliced mushrooms with canned peas.

Use canned asparagus cold for a salad; by itself on a bed of lettuce with a dab of mayonnaise; or mix with canned carrots, peas and beets — plus grated cheese (add cold cuts too) — with your favorite dressing.

What's America's most popular canned sea food? You guessed it — tuna fish. You can invent numerous ways to use canned tuna — everybody does.

The best white meat tuna is called *albacore*.

Don't forget canned *salmon* for a change of pace . . . in salads or as an open-faced sandwich with lemon juice squeezed in abundance.
Also:
mixed with sour cream for a
   cracker or
vegetable dip
for a fish soup
as croquettes, fish cakes or in
   a casserole with noodles.

To a can of PORK & BEANS add some beer and a piece of bacon. Heat on low flame for 20 minutes or so; stir occasionally (while you drink the rest of the beer).

Also . . . make your own *pizza* using a pizza mix . . . but add all the stuff you really like. No comparison with a frozen pizza . . . and it can be good enough for company!

PIZZA

Ingredients to consider:
- Fresh mushrooms
- Hamburger or sausage
- Sliced black olives
- Mozzarella cheese
- Anchovies
- Green peppers
- Onions

In 1954 it was reported from Alaska that a king crab had been found that weighed 12 pounds, with arms that stretched 5 feet from tip to tip!
However . . . in Pilgrim days, it was not uncommon to find off the shores of New England 25 pound lobsters and oysters a foot long! Does that get your taste buds in gear or not!

Make Friends With Your Appliances

Take the time to read instructions. Save your temper, your time and your energy.

Pay special attention to knobs and dials . . . learn *which way they turn* and avoid possible costly repairs to timing mechanisms.

Remember that many appliances have *reset* buttons (usually red). If something fails to operate, try the reset button before calling the repair person.

Quick Dish Wash

A neat appliance to buy for your sink: it attaches to the faucets and has a brush on the end of a hose; built into the apparatus is a soap dispenser. Flick a switch, and water comes out the end of the brush instead of the tap. You can rinse a dish, press a button on the brush to dispense soap, scrub quickly with the brush, rinse again — all in seconds.

Consider buying a *Food Processor*. It minces, chops, grates, grinds, purées, shreds, slices, blends . . . and even crushes ice. It sounds like a wrestler — but actually this easy-to-care-for machine is there to help! There are lots of other smaller, cheaper items you can buy to make life easier in the kitchen . . . including apple peeler, parsley chopper, ravioli-making machine, coffee mill, electric juicer, meat grinder, salad spinner and so many more that a trip to a large department store will amaze you!

Invest in a *deep fry cooker.* You can not only fry things in it . . . you can *boil* in it also, with greater ease than in a regular pot.

Heat water rather than oil. In the fryer basket, cook corn on the cob or almost any vegetable.

Cook spaghetti in the basket, too — it's all ready then to rinse.

Delicious new *quick dish:* coat beef liver or chicken livers in pancake batter and deep fry!

I-LOVE-A-CROCKPOT! If you haven't used one, see if you can borrow one . . . could be just what you're looking for in the way of cook-ahead meals . . . and experiment with it . . . then buy your own!

Try *Short Ribs of Beef:* Drop in 4 to 6 ribs, add vegetables (carrots, potato, onions, whatever), a little water, season to taste, set on low heat when you leave for work; when you return that night — ahhh, ummm, yummy! You have a feast all ready to serve!

Cooking with electricity was first experimented with in England in

1890

... and the Columbian Exposition in Chicago in

1893

featured a "model electric kitchen."

THOUGHT:

As you know, in Japan people remove their shoes before entering a home. A friend tells me this simple practice can more than cut in half floor or carpet wear-and-tear and clean-up time.

"We shape our dwellings, and afterwards our dwellings shape us."

Winston Churchill

YOUR HOUSEKEEPING I.Q.

How many of the following "chores" are you up to daily . . . weekly . . . monthly . . . yearly?

Take out the garbage
Make your bed
Wash dishes
Vacuum floor
Change bed linen
Do laundry
Empty wastebaskets
Clean up after party
Dust furniture
Wax floors
Clean out closets
Fold handkerchiefs
Clean refrigerator

Score:
4 for daily, 2 for weekly, 1 for monthly, 0 for yearly!

Over 40 points = Mr. Clean
30 to 39 points = Above Average
20 to 29 points = Average
14 to 19 points = Still Hope
13 points = Partial Slob
Less than 13 points = Total Slob!

If someone complains about your housekeeping, ask the person to come over next time with a mop!

Don't forget the old phrase "tidying up a room." It's a 3-minute fast-shuffle that replaces *cleaning* when you're in a rush or have a surprise phone call that Aunt Mary or Sweet Sue is on her way over.

Hint:

Have a Secret Sack or a Bilge Box . . . or better yet, a Catch-all Closet into which you can toss everything at a moment's notice — not to throw away but simply to hide for the time being, to be dealt with later.

You can fill in nail holes in walls, prior to repainting, with wet *soap* — if you have no putty or plaster. Let soap dry before painting.

If you have a *small* living room, try putting mirrors on opposite walls to reflect each other . . . and add an illusion of depth to the room.

Remember you can often rent paintings and prints from local museums or art galleries.

more laundry tips

Add bleach to water first and let it mix up a little before the clothes go in.

Close up zippers on pants before putting in washer . . . and turn pockets inside out — (a) to be sure you didn't leave anything in them and (b) for better drying . . . who needs soggy pockets?

You might as well get a *prewashing product* to spray on stains prior to putting a t-shirt or jeans, for example, into the machine. And if you live in a hard-water area, consider adding some *water softener* product — that is, if you really want to baby your clothes!

If it looks like you have suds-a-plenty and they're billowing out the machine, sprinkle on some *salt* to settle the bubbles down!

In the Dryer: don't overload it . . . it slows the drying process and puts wrinkles in permanent press fabrics.

It is better to underdry than overdry.

Clean out the lint trap before every use.

Remove permanent press and polyester material from the dryer as soon as cycle stops.

Avoid "static cling" — there are several products that you can toss in with the clothes . . . or you can stick a "permanent" type inside the dryer drum.

Never try to wash a necktie!

Unless tag says otherwise, you *can* wash an electric blanket.

One friend of mine always buys 2 pairs of the same socks at once; if one sock wears out, he still has a pair (and of course if a second sock wears out, he still has a pair left then too!) To make life even easier, always buy socks of the same color and you won't have to sort them!

If a garment gets wrinkled, try laying a damp cloth on the wrinkle and blowing it with a hair dryer!

Of course, one of the best ways to save time and energy when doing the laundry is to send your shirts out. Try it once and you'll be hooked!

Put a small button under the end of your cellophane tape — and the end won't be stuck down each time you need to use it!

If you get a zipper stuck with some fabric in it, rub the zipper on *both* sides with soap . . . and it ought to come unstuck.

In 1930 food and clothing accounted for 44% of family expenditures . . . compared to 58% in 1900.

Don't collect a bunch of oily, greasy, paint-smeared rags. They can ignite spontaneously. It's best to discard them after use.

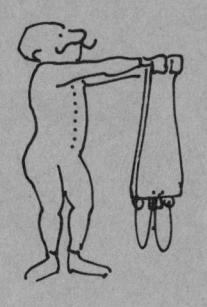

Leather

Take good care of your leather coat, jacket or other leather apparel. Suede, especially, that has grease spots on it, can be attacked by moths and other hungry insects.

Brush suede with a dry sponge or gum rubber eraser. Never put suede in water! Suede shoes can be brushed with a special wire brush — but don't use it on a suede garment.

Smooth or grain leather can be wiped with a damp cloth, or spots can be removed with a mild soap and water solution and wiped dry.

Get professional help for anything more than a slight, superficial stain . . . and be sure the cleaners you go to has experience in handling leather.

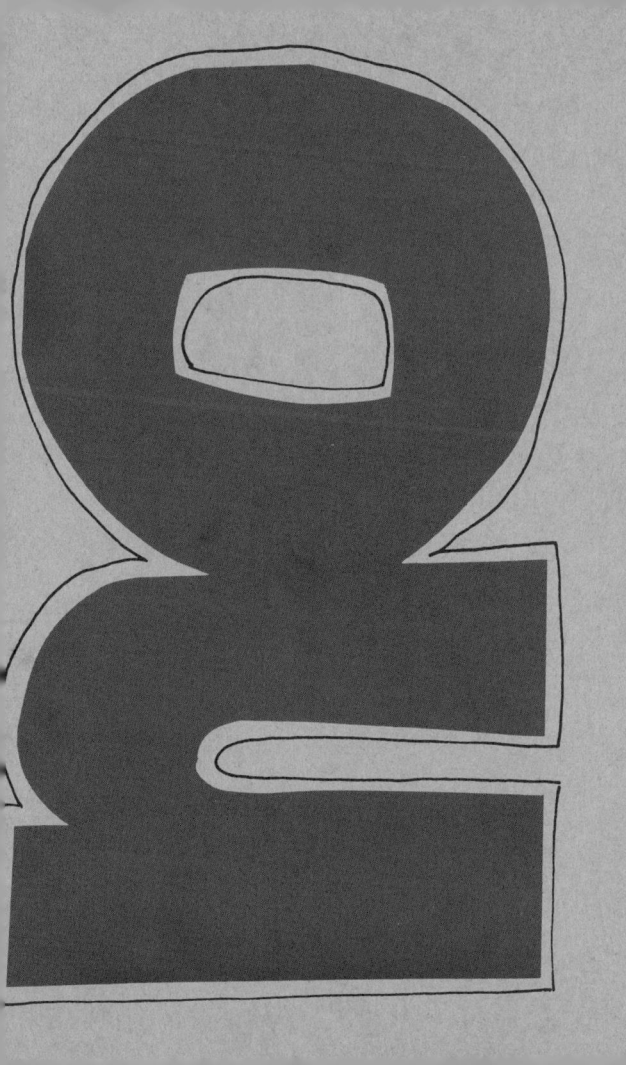

"No civilized man ever regrets pleasure and no uncivilized man knows what pleasure is."

Oscar Wilde

HOME SEC

If you can't afford a sophisticated burglar alarm system, get some battery powered alarms that fit on doors and windows. These may very well scare off an intruder.

Also, you can buy stickers for windows and doors that say your home is protected by alarms; they look very official . . . and the potential burglar is probably not going to take the chance on finding out if the sticker is real or phony.

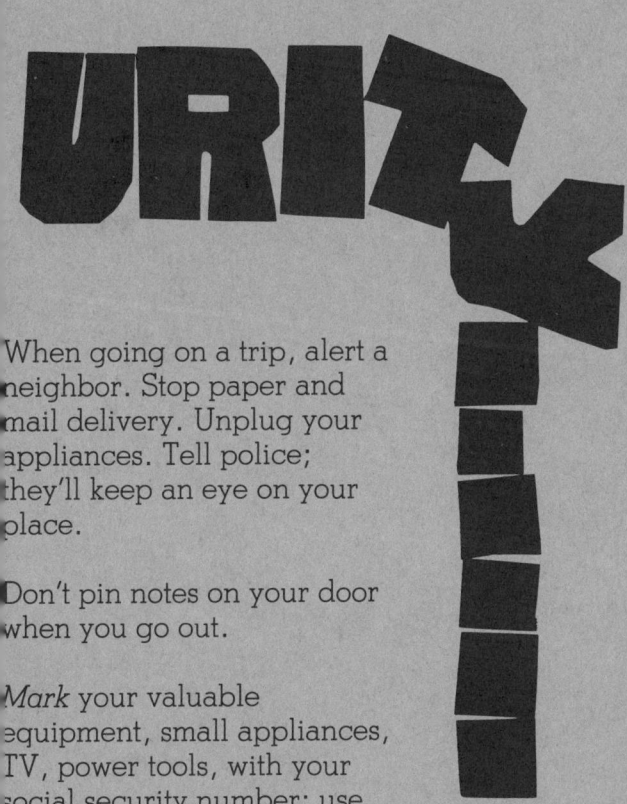

When going on a trip, alert a neighbor. Stop paper and mail delivery. Unplug your appliances. Tell police; they'll keep an eye on your place.

Don't pin notes on your door when you go out.

Mark your valuable equipment, small appliances, TV, power tools, with your social security number; use an etching tool often available from local police.

HOUSEWORK CALORIES COUNT

Check this out — peeling potatoes may replace jogging!

1 or 2 calories per minute . . . talking on phone, eating the meal you just cooked, sewing by hand, resting between jobs

2 or 3 calories per minute . . . washing your hands, peeling potatoes, polishing furniture

3 to 5 calories per minute . . . making your bed, washing windows, scrubbing floor on hands and knees

More than 5 calories per minute . . . mowing lawn with hand-mower, chopping wood, carrying junk up and down stairs

HOUSECLEANING TOOLS:
The Bare Essentials

BROOM: Fiber is better than straw. Store it on its handle.

DUSTPAN: Well, you *can* use a piece of cardboard, but it will drive you nuts never to get all the debris off the floor!

MOPS: Dry mop for dusting. (Wash it once in a while.) Wet mop — use replaceable sponge-head type.

BUCKET: To use with wet mop.

VACUUM CLEANER: Remember to empty the bag occasionally, and keep extra bags on hand.

TOILET BRUSH & HOLDER

RUBBER GLOVES: Optional, but why not look like a pro?

Also: Detergent, ammonia, scouring powder, furniture polish, floor wax. Be sure to read labels and instructions!

If you **forget about waxing your floors**

you won't have to worry about "yellow waxy build-up." Note: On wooden floors an occasional light once-over with a solvent-based wax is a good idea. But with tile, just wash it with a mop.

Remember: In any general cleaning of a room, the last thing to do is vacuum or mop up the floor.

A Thrift store is a good place to buy cheap books if your pad has a bookcase to fill up, even if you're a non-reader and only want the books for looks.

Atmosphere can be important . . . and few things more atmospheric than the *lighting* of your place. Install dimmer switches in living room and dining room especially if you hate to fool with candles or low-watt colored bulbs.

A superstitution says if your shoelace is undone it means someone is thinking of you. Maybe you'll want to trade in your loafers next week!

It's the little touches that count most, according to the bachelors with high batting averages. . . .

Entertaining That

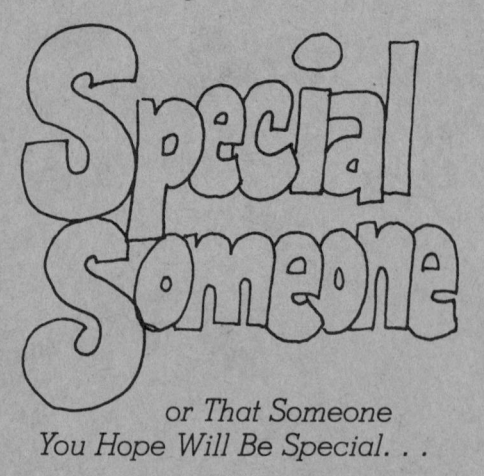

Special Someone

or That Someone You Hope Will Be Special. . .

Have some flowers on the table
Don't ask her to help fix the food
And don't ask her to help clean up the kitchen
Be prepared so that you can spend most of your time with her rather than fussing over the food
Be prepared to laugh at your goof-ups
Put a guest towel in the bathroom

You can, of course, always *plan* a date at your place (with her agreement) in which you both share in all the cooking, kitchen clean-up and other household duties and customs . . . as much as you can get away with!

You can be more than a one-menu male — you know, the guy who comes up with steak, baked potato and salad and calls himself a cook! Women expect a little more these days. Why not become an "expert" in 2 or 3 kinds of meals? This doesn't mean you have to go kitchen crazy! Just decide on a few dishes you really enjoy eating at a restaurant and get a good cookbook and practice preparing them at home.

THE ONE-MENU MALE

Baked Chicken . . . Plain or Fancy

You can use a whole chicken, split in half, or chicken parts.
  Put in shallow roasting pan, skin side up.
  Bake at 350° for half an hour.
  Then brush with fat that's in the pan, add salt and pepper.
  Bake another 45 minutes.
  That's simple!

For *fancy* . . . at the half hour mark, add any spices you like and also lemon juice . . . or other liquid you like such as apple or tomato juice, thinned-out barbecue sauce, a thinned-out soup. When baking is complete, pour liquid (including fat and spices) into a pan, let cool a bit, then stir in some cream and heat to a yummy sauce. Pour over chicken.

Caesar Salad

This takes a little attention — but it's a great "show off" dish to whip up for special female friends! The following is a somewhat simplified version . . . for two.

Use *romaine* lettuce — a small head . . . and a large wooden salad bowl. Ahead of time: make a slice of toast and cut it into small squares (called croutons). Also, add some garlic powder to ¼ cup of *olive* oil.

You will need one egg, salt and pepper, a lemon, two anchovy fillets (or skip if you hate anchovies!), a little vinegar and some grated Parmesan cheese.
Break up lettuce into bowl. Add salt, pepper and olive oil. Slowly "toss" lettuce so that it gets coated with the oil. Add the egg and squeeze half a lemon on; carefully mix again. Next add anchovies, a dash of vinegar and the cheese. Mix slowly once more. Finally add croutons and serve!

It is said that the

ROMANS GREW RADISHES

that weighed as much as two pounds!

A fellow I know cooks for two days every so often, freezes his masterpieces and then eats like a king for several weeks!

If your range has two ovens ... well, I know a flustered fellow who put a roast in the bottom one and turned on the top one. He felt like a fool ... and the roast wasn't too happy either. So ... don't forget to watch those knobs on your stove!

TERRIFICUS!

Try some dried beef in a macaroni and cheese casserole.

Slice some black olives and add them to your next BLT sandwich.

If you're having a cook-out or need a lot of hamburgers fast: roll out the ground meat to an even thickness, then cut out patties with the rim of a large glass.

Add some red wine to meat you're cooking . . . it seems to bring out the flavor. White wine, on the other hand, seems simply to sweeten the meat — which you don't want!

Two touches for soup: add a spoonful of sour cream on top of a bowl of split pea soup; add crumbled bacon (or bacon bits from a jar) to black bean soup!

"Everything which a man *is* depends on what 'e puts inside 'im.... A good cook is King of men!"

Rudyard Kipling

Some beef steers in Japan are fed *beer* to fatten them up!

"The universe itself is but a Pudding of Elements. Empires, kingdoms, states and republics are but Puddings of people, differently made up."

Author Unknown
18th Cent.

A few Words about **herbs** for the man who seeks knowledge and the art of subtlety:

Basil: use fresh or dry, in almost anything (in my opinion).

Bay Leaf: not my favorite — but throw one into stew or with a roast.

Dill: as in dill-pickle. Try with eggs and with shrimp and with most salads.

Oregano: I love it . . . in eggs and with meats and vegetables, especially tomatoes. It's a must with home-made pizza!

Parsley: takes some getting used to fresh (but it's very nutritious). If nothing else, it makes a nice garnish on almost any dinner plate. Try dried flakes in scrambled eggs and in soups.

Rosemary: use sparingly with meats and vegetables, and in soups and stuffings.

Tarragon: a little goes a long way and works well with almost anything. Try with potato soup, cheese dishes and chicken.

Thyme: add to soups, fish, fresh green salads. I like a hint of it with almost any meat or vegetable.

Remember — herbs and spices and flavorings are very personal and individual . . . so experiment to see what you like . . . and how much to use. Always add just a touch and then add more to taste.

"Never cut what you can untie."

Joubert

Good advice ... except in the kitchen, where a man's best friend is his knife.

Invest in some good knives! They're not only safer than cheap knives, they'll save time.

Here's the minimum you should have: a 3-inch paring knife; an 8-12 inch carving knife; a 4-7 inch utility knife; and a scalloped or saw-toothed bread knife.

If you drop a knife, and it sticks in the floor, it's good luck for *you* ... and bad luck for the floor, especially tile or linoleum!

how to carve meat

or how not to look like a real dope. When hosting a dinner — or when you have been invited out and asked to carve — it's great to act like a carving authority!

Here are a few basics: Always use a *Fork* with the Knife.

turkey

Cut off left leg, transfer to separate plate.
Cut drumstick from thigh; slice meat off both.
Cut off left wing. Begin to slice white meat from spot where wing was; work upwards and cut parallel to breastbone.
For seconds, repeat process on right side of bird.

rib roast

Get butcher to separate backbone from ribs (or you'll have to do it).
Use a very sharp knife!
Set roast with ribs to your left (unless you're lefthanded).
Slice from right to left; when knife hits rib, withdraw and use tip to cut slice from bone.

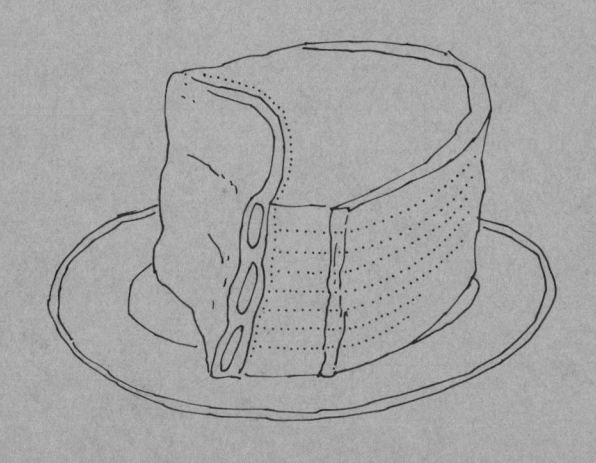

leg of lamb

Shank (with bone showing) goes to your left, thin part of leg toward you.

Cut a few slices from the thin side; now stand leg on cut surface of thin side; shank should point up.

Start from right end, by shank, and slice down to leg bone as many slices as you need; run knife along leg bone under slices to cut meat from bone.

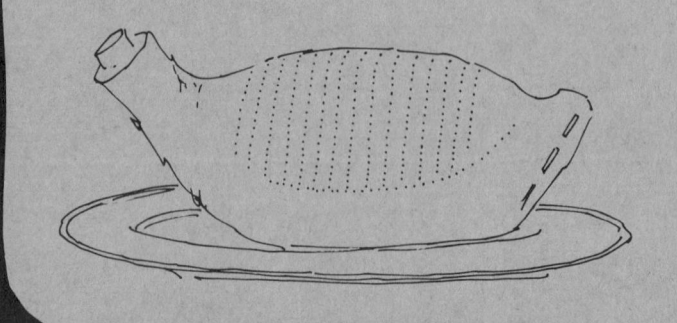

Refrigerator Note: Sometimes it acts like a *cave:* You can lose things in it. You only discover them again by smell. Every couple of weeks check the left-overs and peek into the back of the bins; keep the fridge clean!

Metal ice cube trays: Wash them in hot soapy water from time to time. This helps keep trays from sticking in the freezer and allows ice to come out easier.

When you store ice cubes in a plastic bag, leave the bag open. This keeps the cubes from sticking together.

The first home electric refrigerator was manufactured in America in 1916 (by Kelvinator) ... and it sold for about $900!

when renting a new place

When renting a new place with an existing range and refrigerator, be sure to check 'em out!

Range: Do all burners and oven(s) work? Is the oven clean — or does it look like cars have been serviced in it? Does the oven door shut tightly?

Refrigerator: Does the door close tightly, is the gasket in good shape? Are there shelves or ice trays missing? Is it dirty or smelly inside or out?

Insist on repairs and/or clean-up before you rent.

Buy a potato peeler.
It simplifies peeling!
And, you can use it
to tighten a Phillips head
screw . . .
and as a pencil sharpener.

Use a putty knife
for a spatula . . .
or for scraping off
burned-on and sticky foods.

Aluminum pans
should be *cooled*
before washing
in order not to warp them.

Don't forget
to oil your eggbeater!

Try to keep lids with their own pots — it can drive you nuts when the lid is too small!

Several bachelors I know purchased "dual-purpose" cookware; it is handsome enough to use for serving when company comes.

Don't put a cover on your toaster — or any other appliance. You'll just have to take it off again ... and covers collect dust and general kitchen grime!

Instead of a hot pan holder, use a small sponge to hold a hot utensil, handle or lid. When something drips (or you spill) you can wipe up at once!

An ordinary ice cream scooper holds one-third of a cup of liquid.

YOU'RE CLUMSY

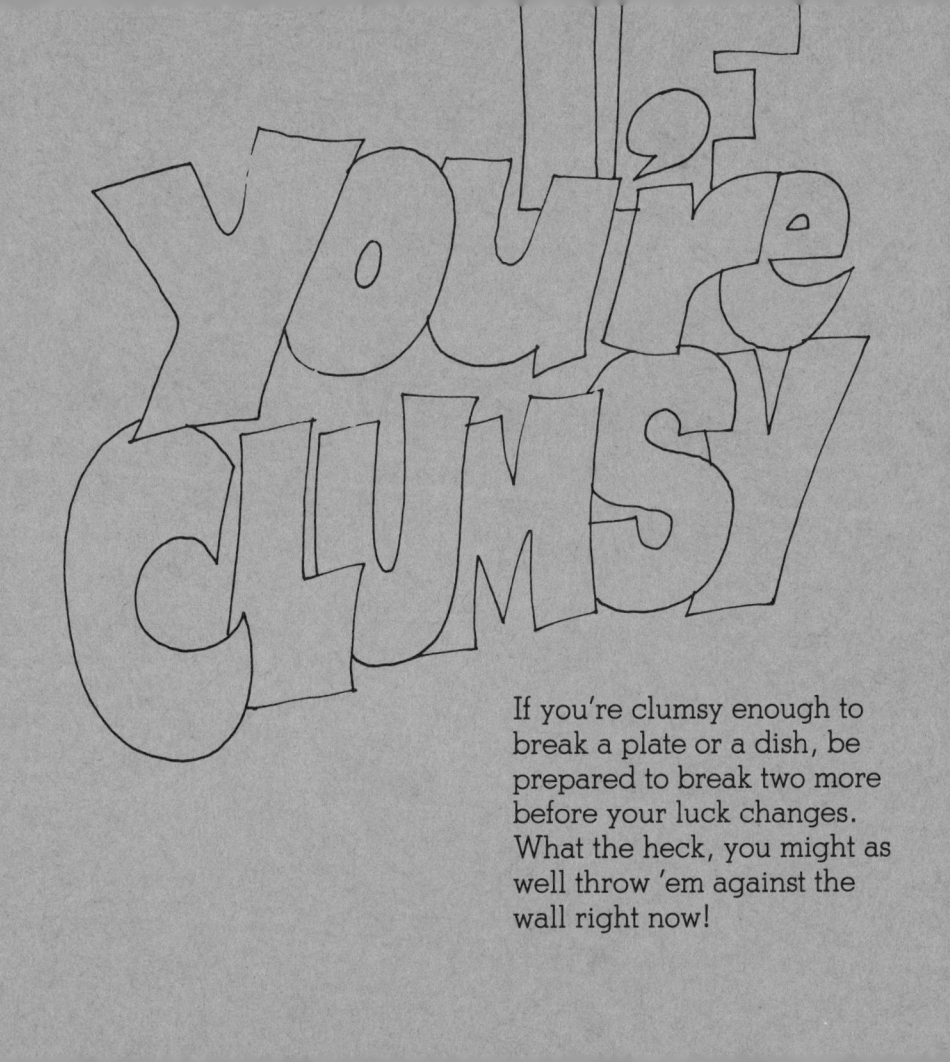

If you're clumsy enough to break a plate or a dish, be prepared to break two more before your luck changes. What the heck, you might as well throw 'em against the wall right now!

You may think you have a good memory, but ... keep a note pad in the kitchen to jot down items you need *when you think of them.* This becomes a kind of running grocery list.

If tap water comes out rusty or yucky-looking, it could mean the Fire Department has used a hydrant on your water line. It should clear up soon. Check before you call a plumber or blame your hot water heater!

A wooden *Knife Block,* or holder, makes a decorative addition to a kitchen, holds 5 to 10 knives — and makes them handier than in a drawer.

Never use hot water on a stain.

How do I get the lipstick out? Try a little hairspray on the fabric before washing. Rub in petroleum jelly or glycerine or salad oil, then wash at once.

Ball point pen marks on shirt or furniture fabric: use a little petroleum jelly, leave on an hour before washing.

Ask your dry cleaners about a non-flammable cleaning fluid to use on your suits, coats and trousers in an emergency.

When buying a new piece of furniture, first figure out exactly where it's going to fit — measure your space and take measurements with you when you go shopping.

I once helped a friend carry a new couch into his apartment. He'd gotten carried away by its delightful size. It looked just right — in the furniture store! No way it would go in his living room—unless he abandoned use of his fireplace or boarded up the door into the kitchen. This particular guy "solved" his problem by renting a new apartment that fit his sofa!

Don't select colors for walls or furniture by looking at a little color swatch. You must try to see the color applied *full size.* A color swatch can be misleading ... and sometimes terribly disappointing.

I've known bachelors who swore by the *furniture rental* route ... especially when they wanted to stay mobile. It is usually cheaper, also, than the difference between a furnished and unfurnished apartment — and you not only can pick your furnishings, you generally get better stuff.

If you like wooden furniture (and especially if you like to refinish it) remember to visit the Salvation Army and other thrift stores. There are still bargains and some interesting pieces to be found.

Thrift stores are full of interesting "junk" to use in decorating (pictures, ashtrays, candle sticks, trays, etc.) as well as practical things that you hardly find anywhere else — such as a really thick iron skillet.

An empty six-pack carton (beer or soft drink) is a good place to keep your cleaning supplies; you can carry 'em around easily and they'll always be handy.

Open windows and air out your place occasionally!

Don't forget to clean your telephone, especially before a party.

Superstition tells us: don't sweep dust out your *front* door ... or you'll be sweeping away your good fortune too. And — if you leave a broom in the corner of a room, people are coming to visit. So get busy — and sweep the rest of the house!

In Puritan times, laws in many New England communities required that single men could not live alone!
And "bachelor watching" was one of the duties of a town constable.

FALL
IN
LOVE
WITH
MASKING
TAPE!

TAPE

Use it to remove lint!
Put it on a hanger to keep
slacks from sliding off.
Use it instead of thumb tacks
to stick up notes.
Put some under the cutlery
tray to keep it from sliding
out of sight in your kitchen
drawer.

When going away for a week or two, water your plants well and cover with a plastic bag (put a couple of sticks in the dirt to hold the bag away from the leaves) and seal it around the planter or pot. Presto — you have a temporary terrarium!

fresh flowers

Get into the habit of picking up some fresh flowers — they'll really brighten your place. To keep *fresh flowers* looking fresher longer: cut a little off their stems each day. Sure, they'll get shorter! So use a smaller vase!

"Animals are such agreeable friends—they ask no questions, they pass no criticisms."

George Eliot

On the other hand

If you want to keep your life simple, don't have a pet. I've never yet known anyone to take that advice — myself included. Sooner or later everyone ends up with a dog or a cat, perhaps a bird, maybe some fish.

Set a feeding routine for your pet and stick to it.

Pay attention to what you feed your pet. Find out what's best for it.

Select a veterinarian to give your new pet a thorough check-up and proper shots.

According to superstition: if you have a canary that won't sing, trouble's on its way! But ... a cat scratching its ear means a friend is coming over.

When choosing a kennel to board your dog, be sure he will have his own individual stall or cage *and* an outside run or exercise area.

"Those who'll play with cats must expect to be scratched."

Cervantes

Make your cat a scratching post: nail a one-foot length of 2 x 4 upright on a flat board one foot or more square; cover the 2 x 4 with a piece of scrap carpeting.

If the metal tags on your dog or cat's collar jingle and jangle, tape them together with masking tape.

If your dog needs to take a pill and won't, save your fingers! Try to coat the pill with chocolate or fudge — which most dogs adore!

Serve your pet on a paper plate to avoid the yucky job of washing his or her dish.

Be sure your dog or cat (or other pet) always has *fresh* drinking water available.

Clean greasy fingerprints or other grease spots off wallpaper with a slice of bread.

Is there an odor in your place that you can't figure out? See if there are any dead flowers still hanging out in a vase somewhere!

an experienced bachelor

acquaintance sets a timer to go off half an hour after he starts cleaning up his apartment. This does two things: it gives the job a definite end in sight (however much he's done) and when he feels like it, he can try to "beat the clock."

Ask your girlfriend for an old pair of panty-hose. Cut off one foot and put it over your dust mop. This picks up more dust . . . and when it gets too dirty, just throw it away.

ALUMINUM

FOIL

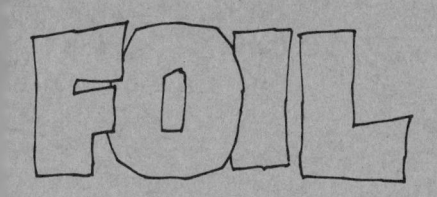

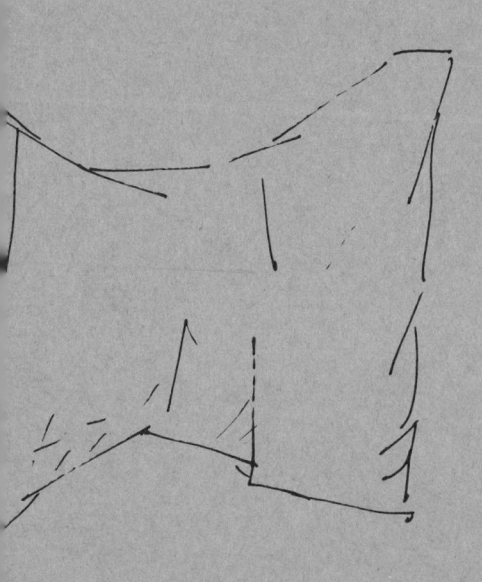

Invest in the heavy-gauge type for wrapping things to freeze.
The regular type is fine for wrapping left-overs and for use in cooking. Follow directions on carton.
Use foil to protect oven and broiler pan and eliminate clean up.
Foil used for wrapping can be smoothed out and used again.
Plug openings in cans of evaporated milk, chocolate syrup and other such items with a ball of foil to keep contents fresh and holes from clogging up.

THE MIGHTY

My old pal Ed's favorite thing is a baked potato with butter, sour cream and chives. He enjoys telling the story about the time a potato blew up in his oven!

Ed forgot a basic rule about potato baking (unless you enjoy dealing with high explosives): punch holes in the potato skin with a fork *before* baking (which allows steam to escape, for you trivia buffs).

Some people bake potatoes wrapped in foil; others think the foil doesn't let the skin get crispy enough.

For a quicker baked potato, stick in a large nail before cooking.

BAKED POTATO

No oven? Oven broken? Just feel like experimenting? You can "bake" a potato in an old coffee can on top of the stove: put some crumpled foil in the bottom of the can, under the potato; put a lid on the can, use very low heat; it takes less than half an hour.

In 1902, each person, on average, ate *two* potatoes per day. Now, the average consumption is only *one* potato!

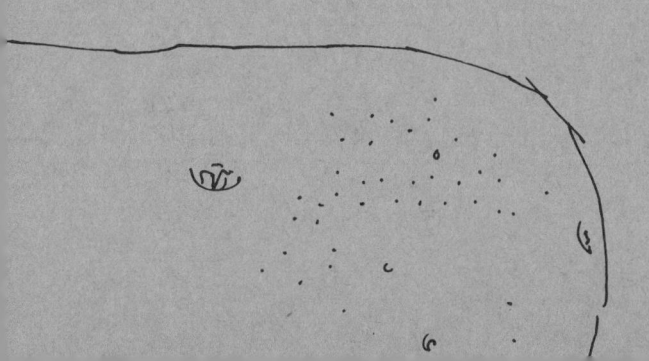

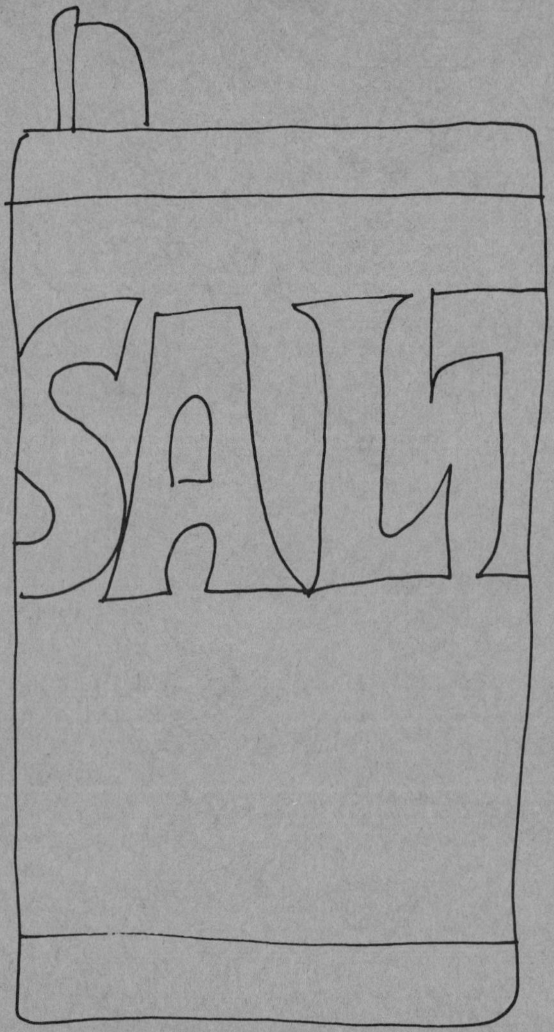
SALT

If you haven't ever done it ...
try SALT

on a grapefruit

throw it on a hearth fire

gargle with it

pour it (with very hot water) down your drains every few weeks

put a pinch in the cream to make it whip better

use it to scour pots with

put some in a little sack and rub on griddle instead of oil when making pancakes!

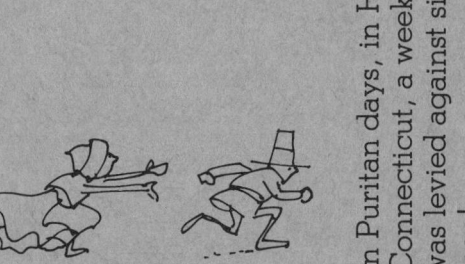

In Puritan days, in Hartford, Connecticut, a weekly tax was levied against single men!

"Such is life. It is no cleaner than a kitchen; it reeks of a kitchen; and if you mean to cook your dinner, you must expect to soil your hands; the real art is getting them clean again, and therein lies the whole morality of our epoch."

Balzac

KITCHEN CLEAN UP

Put the items you keep under the sink in one or more boxes, as needed, easy to pull out and use.

Wooden salad bowls: don't soak 'em and don't wash in a dishwasher. Rinse out by hand and dry completely at once.

Beware of Dishwasher Delusions. I remember when I used to put dirty dishes in with the clean ones (because I hadn't removed them) and sometimes I even took out dirty ones thinking they were clean. Advice: don't leave dishes — clean or dirty — in a dishwasher too long.

soak

Use leftover club soda to wipe off counter tops, laminated tables, stove and refrigerator.

Refresh your garbage disposal! Toss in a few small chunks of used lemon and grind 'em up.

To clean *glass* pans or casserole dishes with brown, burned spots on them,
soak
for an hour in a mixture of cold water and baking soda.

Any time you burn food in a pan, don't try to scrub it clean right away. Soak it in soapy water overnight. Relax. It'll come clean. Soaking, by the way, is my first resort for all yucky pots, pans and dishes.

Consider a small hand vacuum for use on furniture and hard to reach areas. A hand vacuum eliminates the use of attachments (which drive most guys I know, me included, crazy) and works nicely to vacuum your car.

Remember to change vacuum bags when they get over half full, to maintain maximum efficiency. Occasionally clean brushes on an upright vacuum.

You can rent a rug shampooer cheap at your local supermarket.

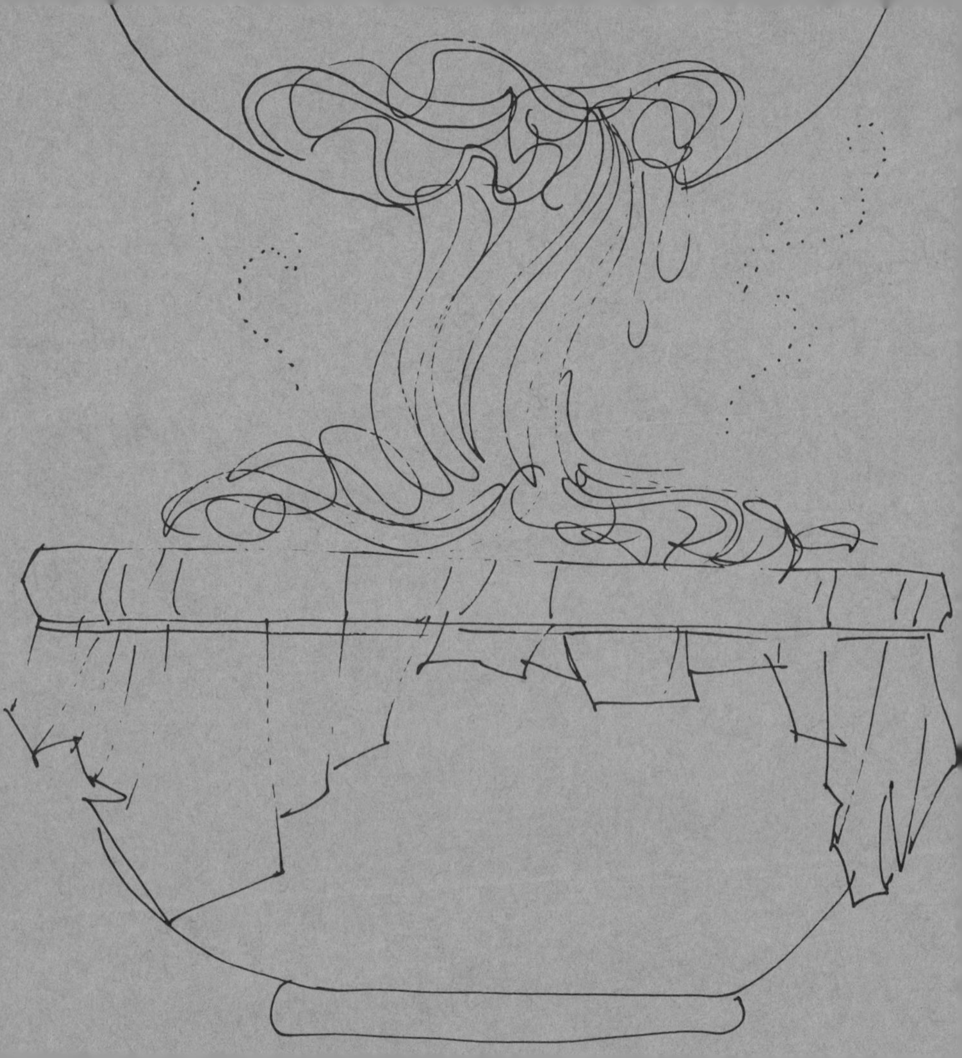

Don't have a colander to strain spaghetti? Use your tennis racket!
Seriously, put aluminum foil over a bowl, punch holes in the foil and hold it on the bowl with a rubber band.

POTS & PANS

Be sure handles are on tight. If they twist or come loose you can spill the food, or worse, burn yourself. If you have wall space, hang up pots and pans instead of keeping them in the cupboard (where you can't see to find the one you need, and where it sounds like Chinese New Year every time you have to drag a pot out from under all those tossed in on top of it).

Use Lazy Susans in your cupboards to hold canned goods (or spices). It's much easier to find what you're looking for.

If you like things to remain crispy-crunchy, like crackers, chips, pretzels ... store 'em in plastic bags inside a metal container (even a coffee can with a plastic lid). If possible you should also store opened flour, sugar, cereals in tin cans (canisters) to keep them dry and fresher ... and so as not to tempt bugs!

Save a few plastic containers (cottage cheese or sour cream or margarine type) for leftover storage.

A peanut isn't a nut at all. It's a "legume" and is part of the same vegetable family as beans and peas.

measuring guide

Dry Measure:
- 2 pints — 1 quart
- 8 quarts — 1 peck
- 4 pecks — 1 bushel

Liquid Measure:
- 16 fluid ozs. — 1 pint
- 2 pints — 1 quart
- 4 quarts — 1 gallon

Equivalent Measures:
- 3 teaspoons — 1 tablespoon
- 4 tablespoons — ¼ cup
- 2 cups — 1 pint
- a pinch — what you can hold between finger and thumb!

Add Spice to Your Life . . .

Instead of . . .	*Try using*
mushrooms	black olives, celery
tomato sauce	tomato paste (watered down)
oregano	sweet basil
sugar	honey
sour cream	lemon & mayonnaise
vinegar	lemon juice
pineapple (with ham)	apples, peaches
ricotta cheese	cottage cheese
milk (on cold cereal)	syrup (juice) from canned fruit
lettuce (for salad)	spinach

Popcorn
For when you have that special girl over to watch the late show on TV:
If you don't have a popper, just use a large pot with a cover. Put cooking oil in the bottom (maybe an eighth of an inch) and let it get hot. Add a layer of corn. Put on top and shake pot over the heat. The popping will start soon; keep shaking the pot until the noise stops. Add salt and melted butter. For a special treat add grated cheddar cheese.

Grilled Grapefruit
Slice a grapefruit in half. Add honey or brown sugar and some butter or margarine. Place under the broiler until top begins to brown and sizzle. Eat with a grapefruit spoon — or cut sections loose with a small knife.

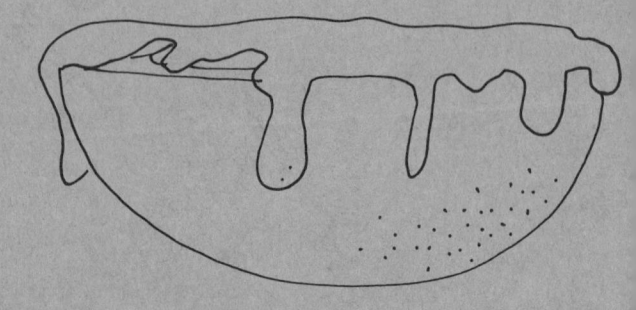

When you grate cheese, brush a little cooking oil on both sides of the grater . . . it will clean off a lot easier. One guy I know uses *pliers* to hold the cheese when he grates, thus avoiding the possibility of losing a fingertip!

Get acquainted with LEMON JUICE. Introduce it to fish or meats (*after* they're cooked), a baked potato, vegetables and salads. When entertaining and serving fish or seafood, especially, put a couple of lemon wedges on each plate.

Try lemon juice in tuna fish salad.

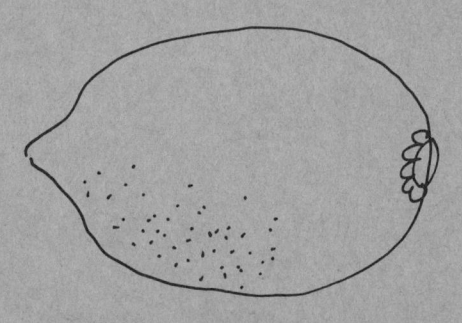

eggs are easy

For extra-smooth scrambled eggs, add some small pieces of cream cheese to the skillet as you start to cook. Use low heat and stir. The cheese will melt into the eggs. Most people will not guess your secret of the smooooothest eggs in town.

Like poached eggs but you haven't an egg-poacher? Cut out top and bottom of a tuna can ... now you have an egg-poacher ring. (To poach an egg, put ½ inch water in pan, bring to boil, drop egg into ring of water, simmer and baste until white is cooked.)

A fast breakfast ...
You can even take it with you in the car! One cup milk, one-half cup orange juice, one egg — into the blender, and into a tall glass. Delicious *and* nutritious!

(MOSTLY) HOME MADE CHILI

(Mostly out of cans!)
Brown in a skillet one pound of hamburger and a sliced-up onion. Add this to a pot along with 2 cans of red kidney beans, a can of *stewed* tomatoes, a can of tomato sauce, and some catsup. Season with as much chili powder as you can stand; add it slowly, from time to time during the cooking process. Cook the chili slowly, on low heat. Add salt or garlic powder or other seasonings if you like. Cook it slowly until it tastes good. I always make it a day ahead of time; refrigerate, then heat up again. It seems doubly delicious!

There's an
OLD WIVES' TALE
that you have to cool leftovers to room temperature before storing in the fridge. Sorry, old wives — but you should refrigerate at once ... unless, of course, you have 18 containers of hot food to put away, in which case your fridge will most likely blow a gasket!

If you butter corn on the cob as soon as you take it out of the pot, the kernels won't shrink ... and remember, mushrooms stay fresher when kept in a paper bag.

If you burn yourself cooking ... run cold water on the burn. Do *not* apply butter or grease. Use a first-aid or burn ointment (which you should have on hand).

Get some cheesecloth to wrap around lemon halves. When you squeeze the juice out, you'll avoid getting the seeds, too!

Coffee Cans

collect bacon fat and other grease

love to have paint mixed in them

hold toilet brushes

make planters (cover them with foil or paint a bright color)

keep crackers and cookies and nuts fresh (use plastic lid)

Honey or syrups that become granulated are okay too. Place bottle in pan of hot water and contents will get "runny" again.

Keep opened can of coffee in refrigerator to retain flavor longer.

Generally *don't* store food in opened cans in the refrigerator; transfer foods to plastic or glass containers to avoid a "tinny" flavor creeping into them.

Don't *nest* glasses; they'll stick to each other.
Also, store glasses right side up so they won't get "stale."
Don't pour hot liquid (like boiling) into a glass unless there's a silver spoon in it; the glass could crack.
Finally — don't sing very high notes while in the kitchen; that might crack all your glasses!

If you have a toaster, clean the crumbs out of it so they won't burn, smoke or smell. Usually you can take off or swing out the plate or tray underneath. Use a pipe cleaner to get at difficult areas.

Never *shake* your toaster — it doesn't like that!

And never poke a knife or other metal object into it.

When you eat a grapefruit, save the hull and use it to clean the sink: turn it inside out and rub it around your sink to remove all sorts of stains.

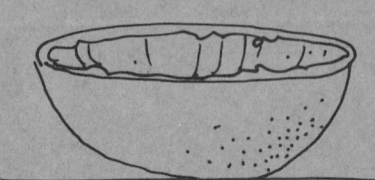

Sink faucets will stay shiny longer (after you've rubbed them spotless) if you put a little furniture polish on them.

Cover your work-counter top space with clear plastic food wrap if you're into some big cooking job — when finished, just peel up the wrap and toss out, with no other counter clean-up necessary.

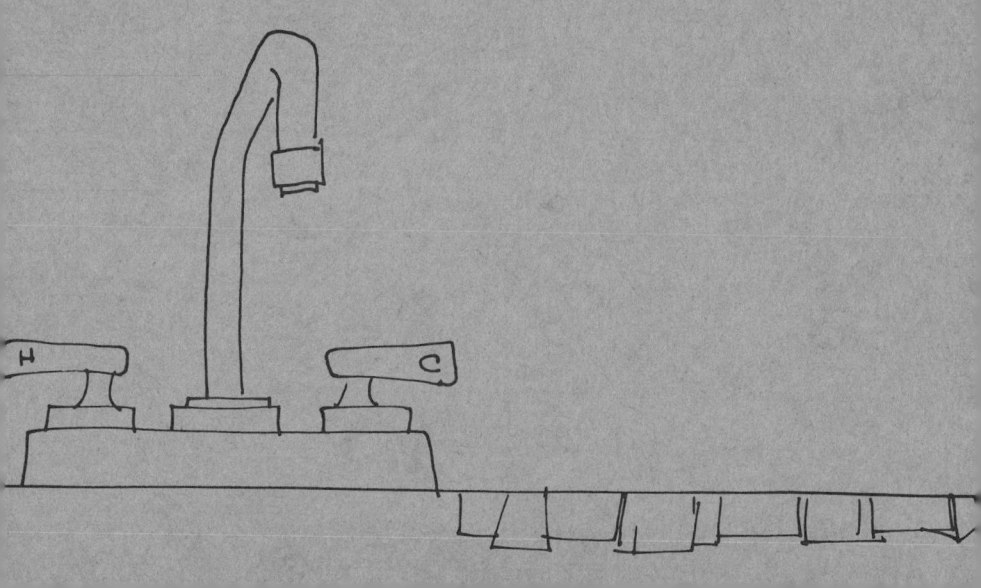

Carry a plastic trash bag through your apartment or house when cleaning up; empty wastebaskets and ashtrays into it, and toss in old papers, magazines and any other debris. Take trash bag to outside garbage can.

Consider planning part of your cleaning around Trash Day — the day or evening right before the sanitation engineers come down your street. It's an added motivation to get all the junk out of your place, empty wastebaskets, remove the overflowing sack of garbage from the kitchen. You know if you don't get rid of it now, it'll sit around another whole week!

TRASH JUNK GARBAGE

Don't bother to buy a window cleaner. Use mixture of borax and water or ammonia and water. Wash windows when sunlight isn't directly on them. Use newspaper or paper towel rather than a cloth, to avoid lint residue.

Before carpet sweepers or vacuums, people cleaned a rug by dropping pieces of wet paper all over it — and then sweeping up the papers, which were supposed to absorb a lot of dust!

Wear a cooking mitt (or one on each hand) to dust with — instead of using a dust rag.

Don't throw out an old hair brush . . .
use it for a scrubbing brush.

Tired of curled-up bacon? Try flouring it a tiny bit before cooking.

Cut the fat in several places around the outside of a steak to prevent meat from curling when it's cooked.

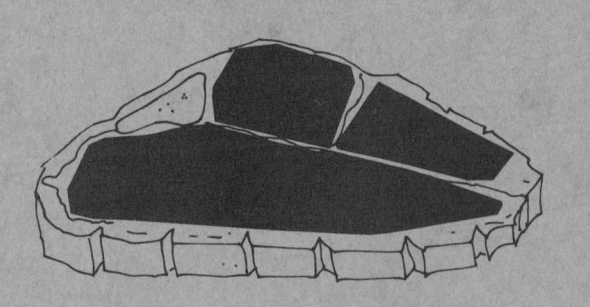

Line your broiler pan with foil, which you can throw away after each use. This avoids a build-up of fat and having to clean the pan very often.

Also, when broiling meat, put a piece of bread in the broiler pan; this soaks up much of the fat or grease and keeps it from smoking and possibly catching fire.

If you're cooking a vegetable and see it's about to run out of water, *don't* add cold water; add hot or boiling water if possible so as not to toughen the vegetable.

How much is a "pinch" or a "dash"? Cooks tell me those references actually mean an eighth of a teaspoon.

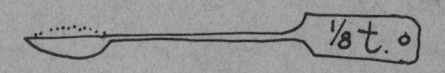

GOOD INVESTMENT:
Teflon-coated, non-stick pots and pans and even electric frying pans. Some people argue the cheaper brands are just as good as the more expensive when it comes to non-stick surfaces. Be sure to use rubber or plastic spatulas or spoons so as not to scratch the surface.

I've never owned a toaster. Instead, I have a "toaster oven" in which you can toast toast — and also quickly fix a lot of other quick-broil kinds of things, from melting cheese on a tortilla to cooking meat.

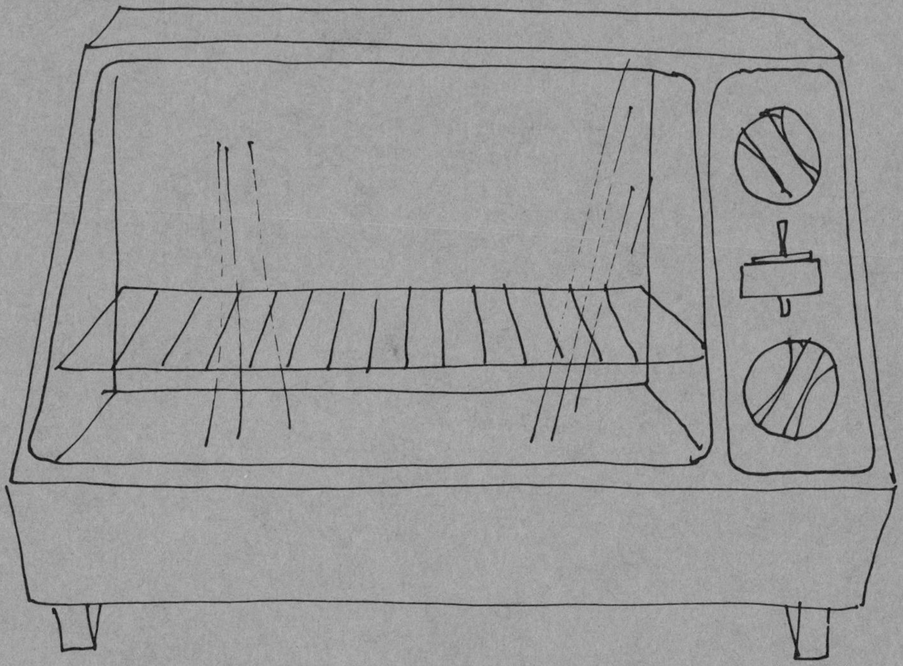

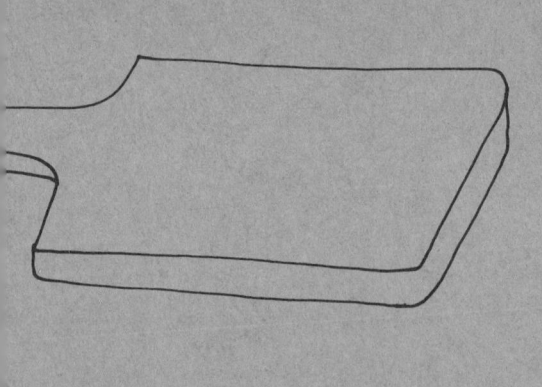

Buy a *Carving Board*. It can come in handy for all kinds of cutting jobs ... and will probably save you from slicing up your kitchen counter top!

Consider a *Wok* ... if you enjoy stir-fried or Oriental cooking. Remember there are various wok tools to get also — from deep fry skimmer and tempura skimmer to steamer rack, rice paddles and chopsticks!

Consider a *Spice Rack* for your wall ... so much more convenient than keeping small spice bottles in a cupboard.

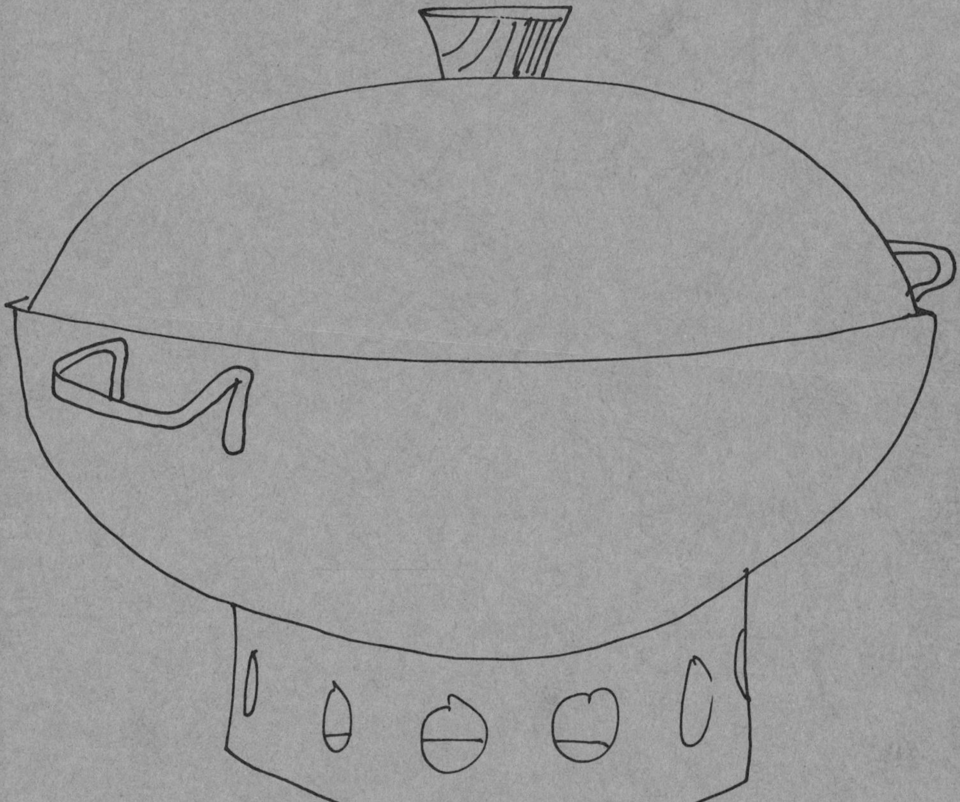

In 1911 a craze for

PAPER BAG

cooking swept England. A man named Soyer seemed to have invented a certain type of bag which allowed expert cooking — a luxury of the rich — to be "equally the privilege of the poor." The paper bag, of course, could not handle the national beverage — tea!

Some people swear by cooking a turkey in a brown paper bag; please get the advice of someone who's done it! When I lived on an island in Europe, the local bakery would cook a chicken for me in a paper bag — in the bread ovens. It was

fantastic!

Tacos

You'll need some tortillas, either flour or corn (they come in packages at your supermarket, keep in fridge). Ingredients can vary, according to what you like. Basically, heat some refried beans. Cook some hamburger with chopped onions. Grate some cheese. Shred some lettuce. If you like avocado, prepare a few slices. If you like black olives or green peppers, use them also.

Heat the tortillas in a little grease in a frying pan . . . don't let them get too crisp, however.

Spread some beans on a tortilla; form it into a "shell," add all the other stuff, as much as will fit. Top with taco sauce — as hot as you like it.

Have plenty of napkins handy!

Quick Pizza Pieces

Toast English muffins slightly. Add pizza sauce from a can, top with grated mozzarella cheese. Broil gently until cheese browns. Cut in halves or fourths.

Crunchies

Mix well in a bowl: 2 cups mixed nuts, 2 tablespoons honey, 1 teaspoon cinnamon and a pinch of salt. Pour into a skillet with melted butter in it, heat on low, stirring constantly until nuts begin to brown. Put in serving dish, cool — and then start crunching!

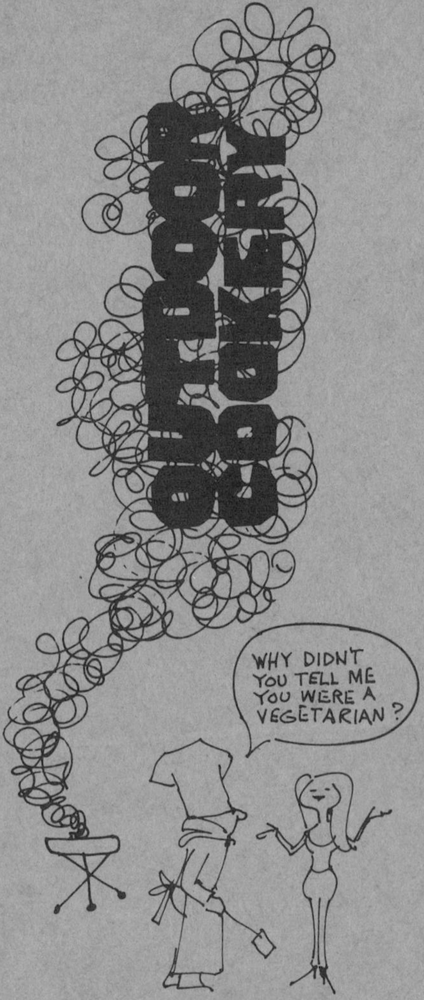
OUTDOOR COOKERY
WHY DIDN'T YOU TELL ME YOU WERE A VEGETARIAN?

Line the bottom of your barbecue grill with foil. This helps the cooking process and makes the grill easy to clean.

Turn a steak only *once* when grilling.

Have a cup of water handy by the grill; if flames flare up occasionally, flick a little water on the fire from your fingers.

Grilling steaks or hamburgers for medium rare, medium or well takes experience. You can cut into the meat to check its doneness if you must — but juice will escape, of course, and it will show you're a novice!

When making hamburgers or meat balls, first dip your fingers in water or chill hands with an ice cube before preparing. Less grease and meat will stick to you.

Brushing a little soy sauce on meat before broiling will give it an added rich brown coloring when done.

THE MAN IN THE ONION BED

I met a man in an onion bed.
He was crying so hard his eyes
   were red.
And the tears ran off the end
   of his nose
As he ate his way down the
   onion rows.

He ate and he cried, but for all
   his tears
He sang: "Sweet onions, oh
   my dears!
I love you, I do, and you love me,
But you make me as sad as a
   man can be."

John Ciardi

Peel and slice onions under cold running water.

Chop onions in an onion chopper.

Onion odor hands? Try washing in milk, rub hands with piece of raw potato or a celery stick.

Buy a jar of onion flakes!

STORE Potatoes & Onions in a cool dry area

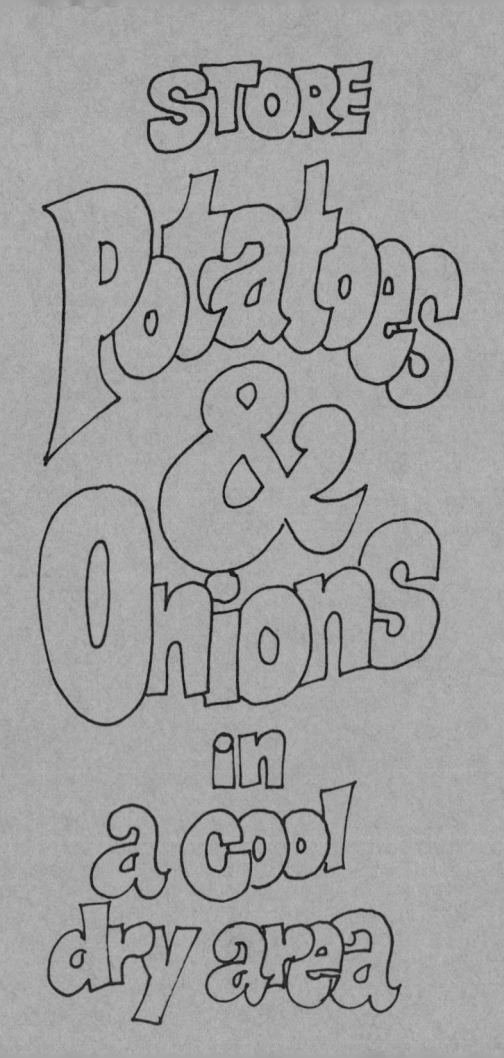

If you boil eggs, add salt to the water to keep them from cracking.

For a little different waker-upper: add juice of a *fresh* lemon to a can of *frozen* O.J. as you mix it with water.

If you store half an avocado in the fridge, keep the pit with it to help keep avocado avocado-green.

In the past tomatoes were known in some places as "love apples" and were not considered good to eat.

Wash fruits and vegetables before eating ... But:

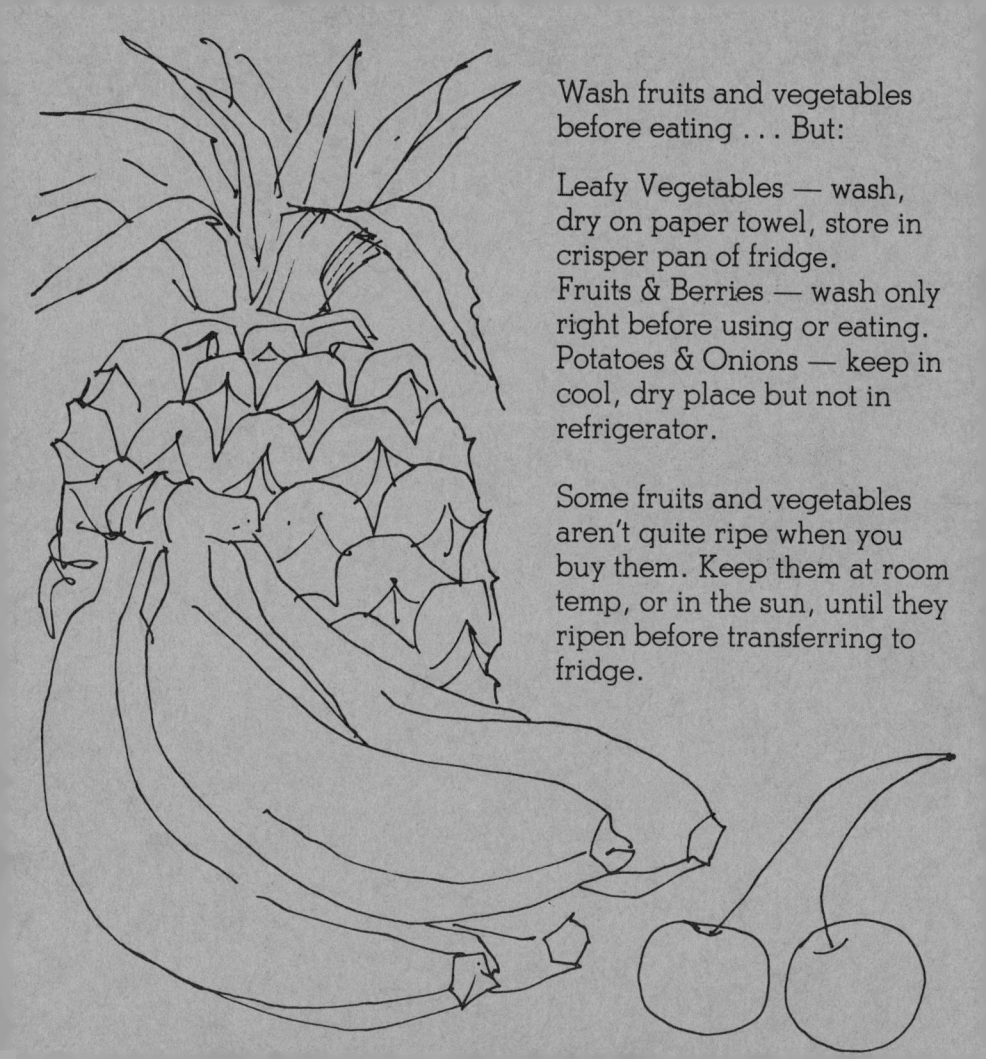

Leafy Vegetables — wash, dry on paper towel, store in crisper pan of fridge.
Fruits & Berries — wash only right before using or eating.
Potatoes & Onions — keep in cool, dry place but not in refrigerator.

Some fruits and vegetables aren't quite ripe when you buy them. Keep them at room temp, or in the sun, until they ripen before transferring to fridge.

Refrigerated Biscuits:

Cut a hole in them, deep fry for *donuts!*

Roll out flat, cover with tomato sauce and cheese, bake briefly for quickie *Pizza.*

Dip in melted butter, indent center, fill with jelly or honey or brown sugar (and cinnamon), bake for *sweet treat.*

Drop in juicy stew 15-20 minutes before it's cooked for instant *dumplings.*

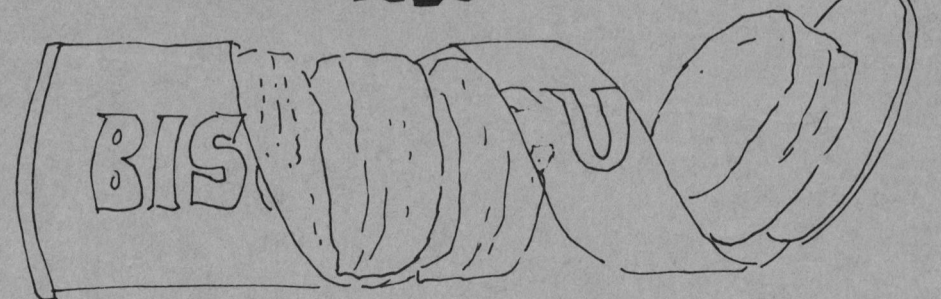

There are about 150 different kinds of *pasta* — that is, noodles, macaroni, spaghetti, etc.

Eight ounces of macaroni or noodles or spaghetti makes 4½ to 5 cups of cooked pasta.

Al dente means "just barely tender."

The major advantage of spaghetti is you don't have to peel it.

Basic Noodle Casserole

After you cook the noodles, you can add all sorts of things to make a variety of casseroles — it all depends upon what you like.

First, cook noodles in salted water. Drain them. In a lightly buttered or greased casserole dish, mix them with a little sour cream. Now you're ready to add the main ingredient(s) — cheese, ham and cheese; tuna, tuna and cheese, plus black olives; onions and tomatoes and cheese (or leave out the cheese); hamburger, left-over turkey, mushrooms, and so on and on. Just mix in the ingredient(s) and then bake the casserole about half an hour (or until it begins to brown) at 375°.

English Muffins:

Toast them, then butter them,
then top them with . . .

tomato slice and scrambled eggs
cottage cheese and fruit
ham or bacon and melted cheese sauce
peanut butter and honey
sliced onion, favorite cheese,
sour cream (broil briefly)

That First Home-Cooked Dinner

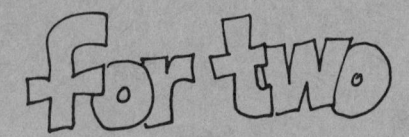

for two

Be nervous, yes — but don't panic! Your latest heartthrob is coming over for candlelight, wine — and a romantic meal you're preparing yourself.

You bought a fancy cookbook and figure that by following directions you can compete with the great chefs of Europe! Well — just remember a few things:

Study the entire recipe first, before you start doing anything. Don't make tomato aspic at five o'clock and then discover it's supposed to chill overnight.

Don't start to make Hollandaise sauce and find

out you don't have any lemons; *be sure you have all the ingredients on hand* before making a recipe.

Also, *be sure you have the necessary utensils;* if a recipe calls for you to squeeze a fresh garlic, get a garlic press (and the garlic, too).

Clean up as you go along. Don't lose the butter or the olive oil or the measuring spoons in a clutter of pots, pans and dishes!

Choose items you can fix ahead of time. Don't be clattering around the kitchen while your date burns in the den; and vice versa! — don't cavort with her while the food burns in the kitchen.

Use a timer with bell or buzzer to remind you when the rolls have risen. Set the table ahead of time.

Consider a trial run: invite your mother or your sister over first!

"Soup and fish explain half the emotions of life."

Sydney Smith

Well, that's one guy's opinion.

"A loaf of bread, a jug of wine—and thou."

Omar Khayyam

That's more like it ... and it's quick, too. No cooking at all!

LIFE IS TOO SHORT TO

tuck in the sheets *all the time*
iron your handkerchiefs
take eggs out of the carton
and put them in those cozy
little cups in your refrigerator
door
hang up your jeans *after*
midnight
rinse your plate after *every*
meal.

About the designer

Roland Rodegast has bached, shopped, mixed, sliced, cooked, served, swept, wept, and drawn pictures of it all.

About the author

When it comes to running a house, Peter Seymour knows what he's talking about... He began cooking and housekeeping almost from infancy (his parents were actors and naturally knew nothing about such things). Then he continued to develop his skills while rooming with three messy intellectuals at Yale University. Marriage set him back briefly, but divorce and renewed bachelorhood quickly allowed him to hone his housekeeping habits to near perfection. Now enjoying wedded bliss again, Mr. Seymour has forced his wife to let him dust, vacuum and mop at least once a week and cook Sunday brunch.

Designed and illustrated by
Roland Rodegast

Editorial direction by Patricia Dreier

Type set in Stymie Light

Printed on Champion Carnival Kraft

Acknowledgments

DOUBLEDAY & COMPANY, INC., for
"A Shrewd Shopper" from *Laughter
From The Rafters* by George E.
Condon.

HOUGHTON MIFFLIN COMPANY,
for "The Man In The Onion Bed" from
I Met A Man by John Ciardi.
Copyright ©1961 by John Ciardi.